Guidebook To Small Computers

by
William Barden, Jr.

Howard W. Sams & Co., Inc.
4300 WEST 62ND ST. INDIANAPOLIS, INDIANA 46268 USA

International Standard Book Number: 0-672-21698-1
Library of Congress Catalog Card Number: 80-50047

Printed in the United States of America.

Preface

How does one select a small computer for personal or business use? One way, of course, is to spend a great deal of time visiting computer stores, computing shows, writing for literature from manufacturers, and reading computing magazine reviews. A second way is to find a guide that will consolidate all of the information on small systems *for* you. The author has attempted to provide that guide in this book. *Guidebook to Small Computers* presents an unbiased view of the currently popular microcomputer systems of every type. Information on each microcomputer has been gleaned to supply a capsule description that includes a factual report of the capabilities of each system.

In addition, this book contains a short section on small computer basics for those readers who are just becoming interested in microcomputers. This introductory material, along with more detailed descriptions of the individual units, should help the reader in making an informed choice of a small computer system.

All of the units described in this book are manufactured by credible companies and the reader will not go very far wrong by buying any of the systems. It is relatively important, however, to define one's goals for computer system use, and *Guidebook to Small Computers* will provide useful information to let the reader determine which computer system fits his or her specific needs.

Chapter 1 gives the novice an overview of current microcomputer systems. There are many features in common among systems insofar as general functions are concerned, but there are several different ways to implement a small computing system in hardware. General software aspects are also covered in this chapter.

Chapters 2 through 11 cover 21 of the most popular computing systems in use today for 14 separate manufacturers. Each system is described in terms of hardware and software. Hardware descriptions outline the keyboard, display characteristics, cpu type, system bus, memory, cassette and floppy disk storage, line printers, and other system devices. Software descriptions cover BASIC interpreters for the system, assembly-language capabilities, disk operating systems, other languages, applications programs, warranties and service, and publications. A summary ends the discussion of each system.

The author hopes that you will use this book to help you select a system. Small computer systems are finally beginning to realize their enormous potential in business systems, data communications devices, programmed instruction educators, and dozens of other applications. If any advice could be given, it is *buy now*! These are not the ultimate in computers and the field *does* change rapidly, but you are certainly missing a great deal of interesting, challenging, and even economic benefits without *some* small computer system!

WILLIAM BARDEN, JR.

To Casey

Contents

1

Small Computer Basics

What is a small computer? What are the component parts? What are the capabilities of an Apple II computer? Is there a disk system for the PET? What microprocessor does Vector Graphic use? What should I look for in comparing computer systems? The author will try to answer some of those questions in the following chapters when we discuss some of the most popular small computer systems available today (see Fig. 1–1).

This chapter will provide a brief description of the hardware and software aspects of current small computer systems. More detailed

Courtesy Apple Computer, Inc.

Fig. 1-1. Typical small computer system.

information about specific computers will be given in the remaining chapters. Although computer systems are becoming more and more integrated into one complete package, they can still be divided into two areas: computer *hardware* and computer *software.*

The division into hardware and software will also be carried over into discussions on individual small computer systems. Specific hardware and software aspects which are not fully explained in this chapter will be described in more detail in the material on the individual computers.

SMALL COMPUTER HARDWARE

Small computer *hardware* designates all physical parts of the computer system including central processing unit (cpu), random-access memory (RAM), read-only memory (ROM), input/output devices (I/O devices), and chassis, cabinets, power supplies, and the like.

Designs

There are two general design approaches to hardware: the "computer-on-a-board" approach and the "bus-board" approach. The computer-on-a-board approach is the newer of the two, made possible by small system components that can be packed into a very small space.

Historically, computer systems have been constructed on a series of printed-circuit boards, as shown in Fig. 1–2. The reasons for this were simple—the total computer system was made up of so many components that it would have been impossible to pack them on one large chassis or printed-circuit board. The result was that the typical computer system consisted of a series of pc boards (also called *cards* or *modules*) that plugged into a "bus." The bus carried all of the common signals for the entire system.

In the early days of microcomputers (the early 1970s) the total number of computer components making up a computer system was still large, and the early microcomputer designs used the bus-board approach. A large printed-circuit board with etched bus lines and connectors carried system signals, and small printed-circuit boards plugged into the motherboards. Each smaller board was dedicated to a separate logical function—cpu, memory, I/O controller, and so forth.

Two of the most popular bus architectures were the S–100 and SS–50. The S–100 bus was the original microcomputer bus and at one time there were dozens of companies producing microcomputer systems or boards for the bus. Because the bus was more or less standardized, any company could produce system components such as memory boards, cpu boards, or input/output controller boards.

Fig. 1-2. Bus architecture.

Another standard bus was the SS–50 bus. Whereas the S–100 bus used 100 bus lines, the SS–50 used 50 bus lines. The SS–50 bus was associated with computer systems based on the 6800 microprocessor, as opposed to the association of the S–100 with the 8080 microprocessor, and later with the Z–80 microprocessor.

Both the S–100 and SS–50 buses are alive and well today, but their popularity has diminished somewhat due to the second general design approach: the computer-on-a-board.

The computer-on-a-board design philosophy is to pack all system components, cpu, memory, and I/O device controllers on a single printed-circuit board (see Fig. 1–3). This is now possible because smaller and smaller integrated-circuit devices pack more and more logic onto a single chip.

Typical microcomputer systems that use this approach consist of an entire computer system on a board measuring 125 square inches

Fig. 1-3. Computer on a board.

(806.5 square centimeters). Many times the basic computer system is in a single unit consisting of keyboard, printed-circuit board, and chassis with power supply, connectors, and other hardware.

In general, the bus-board approach is modular, permitting expandability of the system, somewhat easier system repair, and alternative manufacturers for system components. The computer-on-a-board approach is usually less costly and produces a smaller package for the computer system. The trend is definitely in favor of the computer-on-a-board and this approach will probably become more and more prevalent.

CPUs

The heart of any microcomputer system is the central processing unit, or cpu. In all cases in the systems discussed in this book the main component in the cpu is a microprocessor chip (see Fig. 1–4) that contains tens of thousands of circuit elements that define computer instructions. The four most popular microprocessors are the 6502, Z–80, 6800, and 8080, not necessarily in order of popularity. These are standard microprocessor chips in the personal and indus-

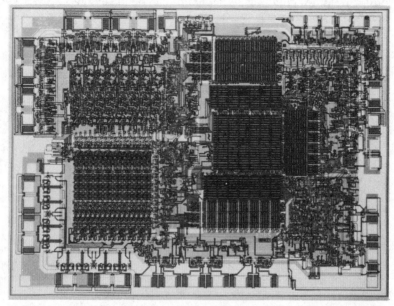

Courtesy Intel Corp.

Fig. 1-4. Microprocessor chip.

trial computing field and are roughly equivalent in terms of processing power and speed.

Each microprocessor chip has other "logic" associated with it to "interface" it with the other system components. Typically, there may be several dozen or so other integrated-circuit chips that are associated with the microprocessor. The trend is to pack more and more of the support functions onto a single microprocessor chip, and, more importantly, to put even system memory and input/output logic into a single chip.

A question that is frequently heard is: "Which microprocessor is best?" A more important question, however, is: "How efficient is the total microcomputer system?" Sales literature notwithstanding, the microprocessor used in a microcomputer system contributes only a small portion of the total microcomputer system performance, and questions about it should be superseded by questions about software performance, good documentation, and system support.

Memory

There are two basic types of memory in current computer systems: random-access memory (RAM) and read-only memory (ROM). RAM makes up the bulk of most computer systems and is used to store user programs for execution. New programs can be loaded into RAM from secondary storage devices, such as audio cassettes and floppy disks. The RAM is used for storage of the immediate program that is to be executed, such as a payroll program or a "space war" game.

ROM memory is a read-only memory that cannot be altered. Permanent programs are burned into ROM and generally come as an integral part of the system on purchase. In general, system ROM contains two types of "firmware": a BASIC interpreter program that permits the user to program in the BASIC language, or a small monitor program that is used to control basic system operations.

The size of memory is measured in *bytes*. Each byte is roughly equivalent to a single character such as *A, 1,* or *. A byte of memory, however, may hold not only character data, but other binary information, such as program instruction codes, constants, or variables. The value of 1024 in one "K," K being a convenient symbol as it is 2^{10}.

A memory size of 4K is 4×1024 bytes and memory size will often be expressed as 4K, 8K, 16K, and so forth.

Input/Output Devices

Input/output devices (I/O devices) are sometimes called *peripheral devices*. They include some of the physically largest and most costly parts of microcomputer systems. I/O devices are used to enter data into the system, such as a typewriter-style keyboard, to print data, such as a line printer, or to store data, such as a floppy disk.

Data entry devices are keyboards, terminals, or crt terminals. Keyboards are very similar to typewriter-style keyboards and operate in like fashion. Terminals may consist of a keyboard together with a printing mechanism for printing data as it is entered. The print mechanism is also used for printing only as results are "output" from the computer system (see Fig. 1–5). Crt display terminals have a keyboard for data entry and display data as it is entered on a television screen. Data can also be output to the screen from the microcomputer. Many times the keyboard and crt display will be integrated into the computer system as a single unit together with the system cpu. Fig. 1–6 shows a typical crt terminal.

Data output devices display data, such as the crt displays described above, or print "hard-copy" data. There are two general types of printing devices. Character printers print data at slow speeds (typically 30 characters per second) and may also have an associated keyboard. Line printers print data at much higher speeds (typically 200 characters per second), but generally sacrifice appearance. Fig. 1–7 shows a representative line printer.

Data storage devices are usually of two types in the systems discussed in this book: audio cassette storage and floppy disk storage. Audio cassette storage uses an unmodified (or sometimes slightly

Fig. 1-5. A printing terminal.

modified) audio cassette recorder to store computer programs or data. The speed at which data can be stored or retrieved is typically 50 characters per second. Cassette storage is also sequential storage, i.e., data must be accessed in sequence; if a program is at the end of a 5-minute cassette, it will probably take 5 minutes to retrieve it.

Floppy disk storage uses a flexible or "floppy" disk about the size of a 45-rpm record to store data. There are two sizes of floppy disks: an 8-in (20.3-cm) and a 5¼-inch (13.3-cm) *mini-floppy*. The most important difference is in the amount of data each can hold. The 5¼-inch disk generally holds about 90,000 characters, while the 8-inch disk generally holds about 250,000 characters. Each type of floppy disk storage device is a random-access device. Data can be accessed anywhere on the disk in a fraction of a second, much faster than an audio cassette. Fig. 1–8A shows the floppy diskette, while Fig. 1–8B shows typical floppy disk drives.

There are many other types of input/output devices for microcomputer systems. A *modem* allows the system to communicate with other computer systems over phone lines (see Fig. 1–7). *Voice synthesizers* can be used to generate voices or other sounds. *Control interfaces* are used to control ac appliances.

Input/output devices can be connected to or *interfaced* to the computer system in one of two ways. Serial devices send data one binary

Fig. 1-6. A crt terminal.

digit (bit) of information at a time. Serial transmission may also be called *RS-232*. Parallel devices are connected such that one byte (8 bits of data) can be sent simultaneously. Serial devices are more generic in nature. There are many serial line printers, for example, that can be directly connected to dozens of different microcomputer systems. Parallel devices usually only operate with one system. A computer system that has a serial or RS-232 "port" can probably use the line printers, terminals, and other devices of many different manufacturers.

SOFTWARE

Small computer software includes the "paper" parts of a computer system. Programs for the microcomputer allow the user to utilize his or her system to perform applications such as inventory, to perform programmed instruction learning, or to play games. Programs may be

14

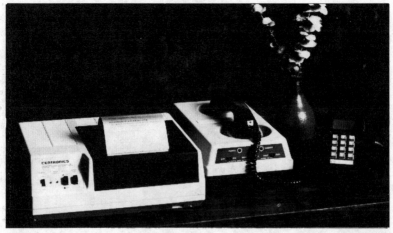

Fig. 1-7. Line printer and modem.

written in several "languages." The most common of these is the high-level language BASIC. At a more rudimentary (and challenging) level, assembly-language programs are used for "utility" programs and high-speed execution. Assembly-language is used to *create* higher-level languages, such as BASIC or other system programs. Disk operating systems are another level of programs that allow a disk system user to efficiently use floppy disks to store and retrieve programs and data.

The BASIC Language

The most common language in use on microcomputer systems is BASIC. BASIC uses commands that are Englishlike in format. To display the line "HELLO, I'M A COMPUTER," for example, one would program the statement "100 PRINT "HELLO, I'M A COMPUTER." In general, the more memory the BASIC *interpreter*, or program that interprets the BASIC statements, requires, the more powerful the BASIC. An 8K BASIC is probably less powerful than a 12K BASIC, for instance. Many of the microcomputers described here use Microsoft™ BASIC. Microsoft is a company specializing in small computer software and has written many of the BASIC interpreters for the computer systems in the following chapters. A typical program in BASIC is shown in Fig. 1–9.

Assembly Language

Assembly-language or machine-language programming is used to create BASIC interpreters or manufacturer's utility software. Users

15

Courtesy Verbatim Corp.

(A) Floppy diskettes.

Courtesy Commodore Business Machines, Ltd.

(B) Floppy disk driver.

Fig. 1-8. Floppy disk storage.

may also use it to create high-speed efficient programs. Assembly language is much more abstract than BASIC and operates at a more rudimentary level. The assembly-language instruction LD A,31, for example, loads a microprocessor register (memory cell) with the value 31. The instruction repertoire for a microprocessor determines the types of assembly language to be used on a system.

At least one manufacturer described in this book, Texas Instruments, does not offer an assembly-language capability for the user on its system. Several other manufacturers do not offer the tools to do efficient assembly-language programming. Fig. 1–10 shows a typical assembly-language program. One of the older such languages is

```
10 '            GETDISK
20 '            -------
30 'PROGRAM TO COPY DISK FILES TO CASSETTE
40 '
50 CLEAR 1000
60 DEFSTR D-F: DEFINT I: DIM D(4)
70 CLS
80 FV=""
90 FOR I=24003 TO 24005: FV=FV+CHR$(PEEK(I)):NEXT
100 IF FV="1.1" THEN IV=26228 ELSE IV=0
110 PRINT@6*64,"THIS PROGRAM COPIES A DISK FILE TO CASSETTE."
120 LINEINPUT"WHAT IS THE NAME OF THE DISK FILE? ";F
130 OPEN"R",1,F: IT=LOF(1)
140 IF IT=0 THEN 560
150 IF IV=26228 THEN FIELD 1, 255 AS D
     ELSE FIELD 1, 255 AS D, 1 AS DE
160 IB=(IT-1)/8+1: IL=IT-(IB-1)*8: IC=0: IZ=8
170 CLS: PRINT@6*64,F" CONTAINS"IT"RECORD(S)"
180 PRINT"AND WILL REQUIRE"IB"TEN-MINUTE CASSETTE(S)."
190 IC=IC+1: IF IC=IB THEN IZ=IL
200 PRINT@8*64,CHR$(31)"GET CASSETTE"IC
"READY TO RECORD, THEN PRESS <ENTER>";:INPUT FX
210 I1=((IC-1)*8+1: I5=I1+IZ-1
220 PRINT@8*64,CHR$(31)"COPYING RECORDS"I1"THROUGH"I5"ONTO CASSETTE #"IC
230 CMD"T": PRINT#-1,F,I1,I5: CMD"R"
240 FOR IR=I1 TO I5
250    PRINT@640,"GETTING RECORD #" IR
260    GET 1, IR
270    PRINT@640,"PROCESSING REC #" IR
280    FOR IS=1 TO 4: D(IS)="": NEXT
290    FOR I2=1 TO 255
300      DT=STR$(ASC(MID$(D,I2)))
310      IF LEN(DT)<3 THEN DT="0"+DT: GOTO 310
320      IF LEN(DT)>3 THEN DT=RIGHT$(DT,3)
330      IS=INT((I2-1)/64)+1
340      D(IS)=D(IS)+DT
380    NEXT I2
390    IF IV=26228 THEN DT=STR$(PEEK(IV))
       ELSE DT=STR$(ASC(DE))
400    IF LEN(DT)<3 THEN DT="0"+DT: GOTO 400
410    IF LEN(DT)>3 THEN DT=RIGHT$(DT,3)
420    D(4)=D(4)+DT
430    PRINT@640,"COPYING RECORD #"IR
440    CMD"T"
450    FOR IS=1 TO 4
460      PRINT#-1,CHR$(34)D(IS)CHR$(34)
470    NEXT IS
490    CMD"R"
500 NEXT IR
510 IF IC<IB THEN 190
520 CLOSE: PRINT@640,"ALL DONE. TO READ THE TAPE(S) BACK INTO A NEW FILE,"
530 PRINT"RUN 'GETTAPE/BAS'."
550 END
560 CLOSE: PRINT@9*64+15,"FILE NON-EXISTENT OR EMPTY"
580 END
```

Courtesy Faulk and Associates

Fig. 1-9. BASIC program example.

```
00100 ;****************************************************
00110 ;*            LP TOP OF FORM DRIVER                 *
00120 ;****************************************************
00130 ; .
F000        00140            ORG      0F000H
F000 3E36   00150 START      LD       A,54          ;9 INCHES PRINT AREA
F002 322840 00160           LD       (4028H),A     ;INITIALIZE # PER PG
F005 AF     00170           XOR      A             ;0
F006 322940 00180           LD       (4029H),A     ;CURRENT LINE
F009 2112F0 00190           LD       HL,LPDRV
F00C 222640 00200           LD       (4026H),HL    ;NEW LP DRIVER ADDR
F00F C32D40 00210           JP       402DH         ;RETURN TO TRSDOS
            00220 ;THIS CODE SAME AS LEVEL II LP DRIVER
F012 79     00230 LPDRV      LD       A,C           ;CHARACTER IN C
F013 B7     00240           OR       A
F014 CAD105 00250           JP       Z,05D1H       ;GO IF ONLY STATUS CHK
F017 FE0B   00260           CP       0BH           ;TOP OF PAGE?
F019 280A   00270           JR       Z,LP10        ;GO IF YES
F01B FE0C   00280           CP       0CH
F01D 201D   00290           JR       NZ,LP30       ;GO IF NO
F01F AF     00300           XOR      A             ;0
F020 DDB603 00310           OR       (IX+3)        ;GET LINES PER PAGE
F023 2817   00320           JR       Z,LP30        ;GO IF 0
F025 DD7E03 00330 LP10       LD       A,(IX+3)      ;GET LINES PER PAGE
F028 DD9604 00340           SUB      (IX+4)        ;SUBTRACT CURRENT LINE
F02B C60C   00350           ADD      A,12          ;ADJUST FOR MARGIN
F02D 47     00360           LD       B,A           ;RESULT IN B
F02E CDD105 00370 LP20       CALL     5D1H          ;TEST READY
F031 20FB   00380           JR       NZ,LP20       ;LOOP IF NOT RDY
F033 3E0A   00390           LD       A,0AH         ;LINE FEED CODE
F035 32E837 00400           LD       (37E8H),A     ;OUTPUT TO LP
F038 10F4   00410           DJNZ     LP20          ;OUTPUT LF TO END
F03A 181C   00420           JR       LP50          ;CONTINUE
F03C F5     00430 LP30       PUSH     AF            ;SAVE CHARACTER
F03D CDD105 00440 LP40       CALL     5D1H          ;TEST BUSY
F040 20FB   00450           JR       NZ,LP40       ;LOOP ON BUSY
F042 F1     00460           POP      AF            ;RESTORE CHARACTER
F043 32E837 00470           LD       (37E8H),A     ;OUTPUT TO LP
F046 FE0D   00480           CP       0DH           ;TEST FOR CR
F048 C0     00490           RET      NZ            ;GO IF NOT 0
F049 DD3404 00500           INC      (IX+4)        ;BUMP LINE COUNT
F04C DD7E04 00510           LD       A,(IX+4)      ;GET LINE COUNT
F04F DDBE03 00520           CP       (IX+3)        ;SUBTR # LINE/PG
F052 79     00530           LD       A,C           ;DIFFERENCE
F053 C0     00540           RET      NZ            ;RETURN IF NOT 0
            00550 ;NEW CODE HERE FOR TOP OF FORM
F054 060C   00560           LD       B,12          ;FOR 12 LINE FEEDS
F056 18D6   00570           JR       LP20          ;GO FOR TOP OF FORM
F058 DD360400 00580 LP50     LD       (IX+4),0      ;0 CURRENT LINE
F05C C9     00590           RET                    ;RETURN
F000        00600           END      START
00000 TOTAL ERRORS
```

Fig. 1-10. Assembly-language program example.

FORTRAN, a language that is oriented toward scientific processing. Another language that has been used for some time is COBOL, a business-oriented language. A more recent language is Pascal, a "structured" scientific language. Not all microcomputer systems offer all (or any) of these alternate languages.

Disk Operating Systems

Disk operating systems are used in microcomputer systems to enable the user to store programs and data on floppy disks. They constitute one of the most important pieces of microcomputer software.

18

There is a great deal of variation in power of the disk operating systems available from various manufacturers; some only perform rudimentary operations while others are quite extensive. A popular standardized disk operating system exists for microcomputers that use the S–100 architecture, CP/M, but there is no standardization among the other manufacturers.

Utility Software

"Utility software" refers to software packages produced by the microcomputer manufacturer for general-purpose system use. Many times utility packages, such as programs to "copy files," "print files," and "disassemble" data, are part of the disk operating system software. Nondisk systems usually have somewhat limited amounts of utility software.

Applications Programs

Probably the most important software for the small businessperson, those interested in computer education, or just the game player, are applications programs. "Applications programs" describe complete packages that perform specific applications, such as inventory, accounts receivable, French-language instruction, math quizzes, "Hangman," or Nim.

Many applications programs are written in BASIC, although some are in assembly language or higher-level languages other than BASIC. Manufacturers vary in the number of applications packages they have available. There is more and more of a trend toward offering all types of applications packages. A good source for applications packages are "user's groups" for the specific microcomputer or secondary software developers that advertise applications. Of course, another alternative is to simply write an applications program oneself.

Documentation

Documentation is an important part of microcomputer software. Historically, documentation has been very poor in the microcomputer area, but it is getting much better. The quality of documentation for companies described in this book ranges from fair to excellent. Many companies are good in describing their basic microcomputer system, but somewhat deficient in documentation for system options.

2

The Apple II

Apple Computer, Inc., created one of the first "appliance" computers in 1976. The Apple I was fully assembled and could be taken home, plugged in (along with the user's tv set), and used minutes after unpacking. The Apple I computer was superseded by a new design in 1977, the Apple II. The Apple II offered a display in color and "high-resolution" graphics. The Apple II has proved to be a very popular computer, second only to the Radio Shack TRS–80 in number of units sold. The color and high-resolution graphics remain two of the strongest selling points of the Apple II. Apple Computer has expanded the Apple II with additional hardware and software products to create a computer system that has application in small business, education, and home use. A complete line of peripherals is offered, including floppy disks and more exotic items, such as modems and voice recognition units. In addition to BASIC, the Apple II can run the Pascal language. Because of the large number of systems that have been sold, there are many secondary firms manufacturing hardware devices, hardware interfaces, and software for the Apple II.

Another strong point in favor of the Apple II has been the corporation's forthrightness with the Apple II user. Information on the system is readily available either from Apple documentation or from Apple representatives.

HARDWARE

Minimum System

The minimum system of the Apple II is priced at about $1000 and is shown in Fig. 2–1. A color television set or monitor is *not* included in the price but must be user-supplied. The computer is contained

Fig. 2-1. The Apple II system.

within a plastic case, along with full-size keyboard. Also included are
several program tapes. The cassette recorder is optional.

The Apple II outputs standard composite video that is compatible
with color television monitors. The video output may also be used

with a normal color television receiver by converting the composite video to a vhf television signal which can then be detected and displayed on the receiver. The only extra item necessary to accomplish this is an inexpensive rf modulator which is available from any Apple dealer. The price of such a modulator is on the order of $10 to $30. The best-quality color picture, especially if one uses the high-resolution capability of the system, is obtained by a color television monitor which costs in the neighborhood of $800. This is usually too expensive an alternative for many users, and a standard color television works fine.

The cassette recorder is a standard audio recorder and will not be discussed further.

CPU

Contrasted with earlier personal computers, the physical appearance of the Apple II is very unpretentious. This is very misleading, however, as a great deal of circuitry and a number of capabilities are packed into the single board of the Apple II. The basic pc board of the Apple II is shown in Fig. 2–2. The system is expanded by adding additional cards that plug into the row of connectors on the Apple II motherboard. The basic board, however, contains all circuitry necessary for a functioning system. A typical "peripheral interface" card that plugs into the motherboard is shown in Fig. 2–3.

The Apple II uses a 6502 microprocessor chip, an 8-bit general-purpose microprocessor. The 6502 is a third-generation microprocessor that has an instruction repertoire of 50 to 60 instruction types. The repertoire is considered to be one of the better microprocessor instruction sets. The clock rate of the 6502 microprocessor is 1 megahertz, allowing about 500,000 8-bit immediate adds per second.

Memory in the minimum system is 4096 bytes of random-access memory (RAM) and 8192 bytes of read-only memory (ROM). The 8K bytes of ROM contain 6K bytes of Apple BASIC, a minimum BASIC interpreter, and 2K bytes of a monitor.

Both the RAM and ROM in the system may be expanded. Up to 48K of RAM may be added to the system in 16K increments. This expansion is performed by adding eight 4116 "dynamic" RAM chips per 16K to sockets on the computer board. The additional RAM chips can be added by the user or by Apple service outlets. ROM may be expanded by adding a more powerful 16K BASIC interpreter, the Applesoft BASIC.

The 6502 microprocessor used in the Apple II allows a memory addressing range of 64K (65,536). This memory is divided up into the RAM and ROM as shown in Fig. 2–4. The addresses from 0 to 49,151 are generally RAM, while addresses 49,152 through 65,535 are dedicated either to hardware functions or to ROM.

Courtesy Apple Computer, Inc.

Fig. 2-2. The Apple II motherboard.

The integral Apple II keyboard is shown in Fig. 2–5. It is a full-size 52-key keyboard.

Video Display

There are two types of video displays available on the Apple II. The standard display provides for 24 lines of 40 characters. Each character is represented by a 5 by 7 dot matrix in one character position. Normal (white on black) or "reverse" (black on white) video or flashing characters can be represented. The standard display also allows color graphics. Fifteen colors can be represented and displayed as a matrix of 40 horizontal and 48 vertical elements.

23

Courtesy Apple Computer, Inc.

Fig. 2-3. Apple II interface card.

The second type of video display is high-resolution graphics. This feature is software controlled and loaded as a separate program. High-resolution graphics provides four colors—black, white, green, and purple. In this mode the display is divided into a matrix of 280 horizontal by 192 vertical elements. The total number of elements with this option is therefore 53,760, which allows for a fine resolution of graphics to create animation or detail. The graphics and display capabilities are shown in Fig. 2-6.

Cassette Storage

The cassette interface logic is also present on the Apple II motherboard. It uses a normal audio cassette recorder to save programs or data. Data can be transferred between cassette tapes and the Apple II at rates of 1500 bits per second, or about 187.5 bytes per second. A 4096-byte program can be loaded in about 22 seconds.

Other Standard Input/Output

Also on the basic Apple II motherboard are a speaker and "game" I/O connector. The speaker can be programmed under software control (BASIC or assembly language) to create music or sound effects. The game I/O connector allows for connection of four game paddles; two paddles are supplied with the system. The game paddles are essentially analog-to-digital converters (the game paddles are poten-

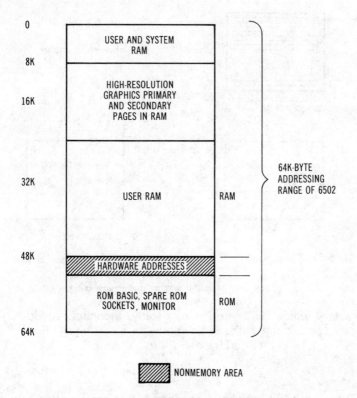

Fig. 2-4. Apple II memory mapping.

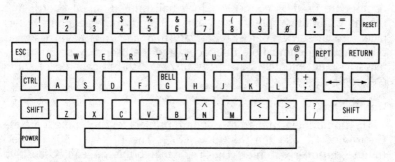

Fig. 2-5. Apple II keyboard layout.

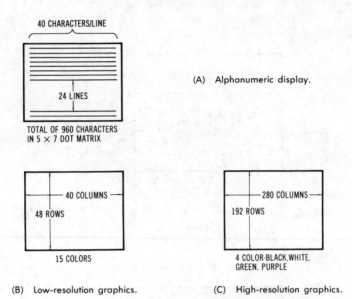

(A) Alphanumeric display.

40 CHARACTERS/LINE

24 LINES

TOTAL OF 960 CHARACTERS
IN 5 × 7 DOT MATRIX

40 COLUMNS

48 ROWS

15 COLORS

(B) Low-resolution graphics.

280 COLUMNS

192 ROWS

4 COLOR-BLACK,WHITE,
GREEN, PURPLE

(C) High-resolution graphics.

Fig. 2-6. Apple II display characteristics.

tiometers) which can be read under software control. In addition to
the four paddle inputs the game connector has three additional "discrete" inputs and four additional discrete outputs.

System Bus

There are eight peripheral connectors that are mounted near the
back edge of the Apple II motherboard. Each one of these connects to
the system bus lines. The signals on the system bus lines are identical
with or related to the signals from the 6502 microprocessor (8 data
lines, 16 address lines, and control signals). The eight peripheral connectors are used as connectors for small printed-circuit boards that
mount within the Apple II case itself. Standard Apple peripheral interfaces use these pc boards, secondary manufacturers have designed
other Apple II compatible interfaces, and the user may design interfaces to plug into the system bus if he or she is capable of some
electronic design.

Line Printers

The line printers offered as standard printers for the Apple II are the
Centronics P1 and the Centronics 779. The P1 is a 150 line-per-
minute dot-matrix printer (Fig. 1–7) that prints on electrosensitive
paper (aluminized). The 779 is a larger printer (see Fig. 2–7) that

Fig. 2-7. Apple II peripherals.

prints full-size forms at 60 characters per second on ordinary printer paper. Both units are supplied with a parallel printer interface card which plugs into one of the eight peripheral connectors in the Apple.

A number of other printers can easily be interfaced to the Apple by using the parallel printer interface card option. The signals supplied by the card can be easily modified to make them compatible with many microcomputer printers currently available. An alternate approach is to use the optional serial interface card to connect "serial" printers. The serial card will also interface communications devices such as modems.

Disk Drives

The standard disk used with the Apple II is a Shugart SA400 5¼-inch (13.3-cm) floppy disk drive (Fig. 2–7). Here again, a disk controller card plugs into a peripheral connector within the Apple. Each disk controller card controls two drives, and the maximum number of drives that could conceivably be used is 14 for about 1.6 megabytes of data. (Each diskette can store about 90,000 bytes of data.)

Other Input/Output Devices

Apple offers a number of other input/output devices, including a voice recognition unit, an ac line control unit for controlling ac appliances or devices, and an originate/answer modem (see Fig. 2–7) for telephone data communications. In addition to standard Apple devices, however, there are a large number of secondary manufacturers that offer input/output devices complete with interface, such as plotters, digitizers, and real-time clocks.

SOFTWARE

Apple BASIC and Applesoft BASIC

There are two versions of BASIC that are available for the Apple II computer. Apple II BASIC is a 6K BASIC that is resident in ROM in the minimum configuration Apple II system. It is an *integer* BASIC, meaning that it does not allow mixed numbers or very large or small numbers (the number range is −32,768 to +32,767). It is a fast BASIC and perfectly suitable for some applications, such as game playing or limited processing. It is not a general-purpose BASIC, however.

Applesoft BASIC (a combination of *Apple* and Micro*soft,* the developer of the BASIC) *is* a general-purpose BASIC. It requires 16K and can be either loaded from cassette tape or purchased as a ROM resident program. Both the Apple II BASIC and Applesoft BASIC contain a number of commands to support the low-resolution graphics of the system.

Assembly Language

The minimum Apple II system contains a 2K-byte monitor that is resident in ROM. This monitor allows the user to do limited assembly of machine language programs. It also provides debug capability such as examining data in memory, modifying data, and "break-pointing" (stopping at a predetermined instruction).

A full-fledged assembler for the Apple is not currently available from the manufacturer, but one is available from a number of other sources.

Disk II Operating System

Apple offers the Disk II floppy disk subsystem for the Apple II. It consists of a disk controller card, one or two mini-floppy disk drives, and DOS, or disk operating system. The DOS software allows programs and data to be stored on floppy disk and permits copying, deletion, or renaming of files by name. Random or sequential file access is allowed.

Applications Programs

As there are a large number of Apples that have been sold, there is a wide range of Apple II applications programs. These are primarily available from secondary software developers, although Apple has a number of applications programs under development.

Current applications from Apple, Inc., include a stock reporter, finance package, and checkbook program in addition to games programs. Software from other sources includes many games, such as chess and bridge, and some business-oriented applications packages.

Pascal

A strong selling point for Apple is the availability of the Pascal language for the Apple II. The minimum Apple system required for Pascal is 48K of RAM memory, one disk drive, and the Pascal software package. Apple Pascal consists of a screen-oriented editor, a filer (disk file manage), system utilities, and the Pascal compiler which uses "standard" Pascal plus extensions for high-resolution graphics and other functions.

WARRANTIES AND SERVICE

As most computer stores carry the Apple II and there are currently 1200 or so computer stores, Apple service is easier to find than service on many other small computers. The Apple II has a 90-day warranty for parts and labor, and extended warranties are available.

PUBLICATIONS

Apple publications (see Fig. 2–8) are well written and complete insofar as the Apple II Reference Manual and Applesoft manuals are concerned. Other options are not documented as well.

Courtesy Apple Computer, Inc.

Fig. 2-8. Apple publications.

Chart 2-1. Apple II Summary

Model: Apple Computer, Inc., Apple II Computer System

HARDWARE

Microprocessor:	6502.
Bus, Architecture:	Own bus design. Motherboard with plug-in interfaces.
Keyboard:	Integral full-size keyboard.
Television Monitor:	None. User-supplied color receiver or monitor.
Cassette Recorder:	Optional item. About 150 bytes per second.
Line Printer:	Centronics P1 or 779 offered by Apple. Others compatible.
Disk Drives:	Mini-floppy drives hold 90,000 bytes. Up to 14.
Modem:	Available.
Other Peripheral Devices:	Voice recognition unit, ac control unit, others. Joysticks and interface included.
Serial, Parallel Ports:	Through addition of peripheral cards.

SOFTWARE

BASIC Interpreter:	6K resident BASIC (integer). 16K BASIC loaded from tape or disk.
Assembly Language:	Machine-language programming through monitor. Assembler available.
Other Languages:	Pascal available.
Disk Operating System:	Available.
Utility Programs:	Large number, primarily through secondary suppliers.
Applications Programs:	Large number, primarily through secondary suppliers.
User Group Activity:	Very active. Meetings in metropolitan areas.
Publications:	Fair to good.
Warranties, Repair:	90 days. Local repair available.

SUMMARY

The Apple II is a well-designed, compact, personal computer with a large following. It has excellent color graphics and control functions, is being used as a business computer, and has local service available. Chart 2–1 provides a summary of Apple II hardware and software features.

3

Atari Computers

Atari, Inc., is an established electronic game manufacturer well known for its PONG and other video games. Atari and other companies have been expanding their video games from "dedicated" electronic devices to systems which can play many types of games by loading a new game from a cassette tape package or, in some cases, by a read-only-memory cartridge. Of course, not only games but many different types of applications can be loaded in this type of system—educational packages, home applications, and others.

In 1979, Atari introduced its Atari 400 and 800 personal computer systems. Far from being just an upgraded video game, the new computers are equivalent to many existing personal computer systems with color graphics, an optional line printer, and optional floppy disk drives. What is more, Atari is strongly emphasizing educational software for their computers, with hundreds of software applications packages completed or planned.

HARDWARE

Atari has two personal computers: the Atari 400 (Fig. 3–1A) and Atari 800 (Fig. 3–1B). The basic architecture and physical layout of the systems are the same, but the Atari 400 is a low-cost version of the 800 (about $550).

Atari 400

The Atari 400 is a single-chassis computer with integral keyboard. The keyboard is a "panel" type without discrete keys that operates by capacitive touch. It has 57 keys, including upper and lower case and four "function keys" that are dedicated to system control functions (see Fig. 3–2). The system does not come with a built-in television monitor; the user's own color television receiver is used for that purpose. The 400 comes with an "rf modulator" which converts the composite video produced by the system into an rf signal that can be utilized by the television receiver.

The 400 has two means of entering programs for execution: cartridges and cassette tape. The cartridge method is a standard feature with the system, while the cassette tape device is an audio cassette recorder option. The cartridges are actually read-only-memory (ROM) devices that plug into the system with preprogrammed software applications.

The Atari 400 incorporates a 6502 microprocessor chip. The 6502 is a third-generation microprocessor that is used in many of the microcomputers discussed in this book. The clock rate of the 6502 is 1 megahertz, permitting 500,000 8-bit immediate adds per second.

The system also includes several other very-large-scale integrated circuits, including a programmable display microcontroller chip for high-resolution color graphics.

Memory in the 400 is divided into read-only memory (ROM) and random-access memory (RAM). The ROM is 8192 (8K) bytes of built-in memory that contains a BASIC interpreter program. The BASIC interpreter decodes BASIC program statements in the plug-in ROM cartridges from cassette programs that have been loaded or from user programs entered from the keyboard. ROM cartridges extend the ROM memory area from 8K to 16,384 (16K) bytes as individual cartridges are loaded.

RAM is a fixed 8192 (8K) bytes in the 400 system, and is not expandable. The RAM area holds user programs loaded from cassette or entered from the keyboard.

The 400 displays characters or graphics in high-resolution color. There are eight different modes of displays in the system and up to 16 colors that may be programmed. The basic display mode displays 12 lines of 38 characters each, as shown in Fig. 3–3A. In this mode both uppercase and lowercase characters may be displayed in addition to graphics characters. The graphics characters are entered from the keyboard and include line segments and special game characters.

The other display modes allow display of high-density graphics points ranging from 39 columns by 20 rows to 158 columns by 80 rows. The highest resolution, therefore, allows 12,640 individual "pixels" which may be programmed to different colors.

The 400 comes with a built-in speaker and four "audio channels." Each of the channels may be separately programmed for tone and volume. This is quite a powerful feature not usually found on microcomputer systems, and it permits synthesizing four musical voices to play four-part harmony!

Another feature of the 400 is the capability to add four "joystick" controllers. The interface exists in the system, and it is only necessary to add the optional joystick units for many game packages.

The optional cassette recorder is basically a custom audio cassette recorder designed with two tracks, one for audio and one for digital data. The digital track transfers data at rates of either 30 or 60 characters per second. The audio track is used in conjunction with Atari's

(A) Atari 400.

Fig. 3-1. Atari

cassette educational programs. BASIC programs can be created from the keyboard, of course, and stored on cassette.

Atari 800

The 800 is an expandable version of the 400. It can be upgraded to more random-access memory (RAM), a line printer, disc drives, and other options. The basic unit costs about $1000.

Courtesy Atari, Inc.

(B) Atari 800.

systems.

(A) Basic keyboard layout.

(B) Keyboard-controlled graphics characters.

Courtesy Atari, Inc.

Fig. 3-2. Atari 400/800 keyboard layout.

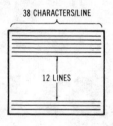

(A) Alphanumeric mode: 12
lines of 38 characters/line =
456 characters in 16 colors.

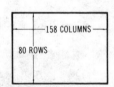

(B) Highest-resolution graphics
mode.

Fig. 3-3. Atari display characteristics.

The keyboard in the 800 is a full-size 57-key keyboard with the same basic layout as the 400. The keys are discrete keys which, in general, have a better "tactile" response than the panel-type keyboard of the 400.

As in the 400, the 800 has an rf modulator, internal speaker, and cartridge slots for ROM cartridges. The display modes are identical with the modes discussed for the 400. The cassette recorder is also identical with the one optionally available for the 400. In this case the recorder is included in the 800 package. The digital track of the recorder transfers data at rates of 60 characters per second.

Internally the 800 uses the same microprocessor and LSI chips as the 400—a 6502 microprocessor and graphics generator. RAM is expandable in the 800, however. The basic 800 comes with one 8192- (8K-) byte RAM module and one 10,240- (10-K) byte ROM module, the ROM module containing the BASIC interpreter and monitor. RAM may be increased by adding 8K or 16K RAM modules up to a total of 48K. Plug-in ROM cartridges may also be used in lieu of cassette programs.

The 800 has a number of peripheral devices that may be added to the system. The first of these is the system line printer (about $600) shown in Fig. 3–1B. This is a 1000 line-per-minute 5-by-7 dot-matrix printer. Lines are 40 characters wide. The printer uses standard 3 7/8-inch-wide (9.8-cm) roll paper.

The second 800 option is a floppy-disk drive unit (about $750) also shown in the same figure. This is a mini-floppy drive that uses 5¼-inch (13.3-cm) diskettes. Storage on each diskette is about 88K bytes. Up to four disk drives may be used in the system.

Other options that will be available are an acoustic modem, screen light pen, and program recorder. The light pen option can be used to select screen coordinates, characters, or fields for interaction with the program. A program recorder option allows programs to be recorded on ROM.

SOFTWARE

The Atari systems are oriented towards BASIC and applications programs written in BASIC. The BASIC is an 8K BASIC that has all of the "extensions" for use on the Atari systems to permit graphics displays in color, programming the audio channels, and joystick control. Atari also has assembly-language capability and assembly-language utilities. One of the ROM cartridges contains an assembler/debug package for 6502 assembly-language program development. The disk drive systems include a DOS disk operating system that has rudimentary file management.

As was mentioned earlier, Atari has, or will have, many educational cassette programs. These present text, pictures, and multiple choice questions, and are accompanied by narration on the cassette recorder. Each program set is priced at about $40. ROM cartridges for the system include programs such as chess, music composition, and games and are priced somewhat higher.

Chart 3-1. Atari 400/800 Summary

Model: Atari 400/800 Personal Computer Systems

HARDWARE

Microprocessor:	6502.
Bus, Architecture:	Own bus design. Plug-in modules.
Keyboard:	Integral, full-size, keyboard-panel type on 400.
Television Monitor:	None. User-supplied color television receiver.
Cassette Recorder:	Optional on 400, standard on 800. About 60 bytes per second.
Line Printer:	1000 line/minute dot matrix. 40 characters/line.
Disk Drives:	Mini-floppy drives hold 88K bytes. Up to 4.
Modem:	Will be available.
Other Peripheral Devices:	Screen light pen, program recorder will be available. Joysticks available as option.
Serial, Parallel Ports:	None.

SOFTWARE

BASIC Interpreter:	8K resident BASIC interpreter.
Assembly Language:	Assembler/debug package available.
Other Languages:	None.
Disk Operating System:	Provided with disk drives.
Utility Programs:	Some.
Applications Programs:	Many available currently or planned.
User Group Activity:	None currently, due to newness of product.
Publications:	Fair. Good BASIC manual.
Warranties, Repair:	90 days. Undefined service at present.

WARRANTIES AND SERVICE

Atari products carry a 90-day warranty for parts and labor. Service facilities are undefined at this time of writing.

SUMMARY

The Atari systems are excellent personal computer systems for the programming novice. The computers appear to be very well designed, and the integral audio and joystick ports are options not usually found on microcomputers. The high-resolution color graphics and other features make the Atari systems very competitive with existing systems such as the Apple II or OSI C4P. Chart 3–1 provides a summary of Atari hardware and software features.

4

The Commodore PET

Commodore Business Machines, Ltd., introduced a truly inexpensive "appliance" computer in 1977—the PET 2001. The PET (*Personal Electronic Transactor*) was the lowest-priced ($600) fully integrated personal computer at its time of introduction and still remains a good bargain in terms of performance versus price. The original PET 2001 system consists of a cpu with keyboard, built-in cassette, and attached black-and-white video monitor. The newer PET has a larger keyboard (the original was not full-sized), some redesigning of the electronics, and a requirement of an external cassette (see Fig. 4–1).

Commodore has expanded the new PET into a complete business and applications system with floppy disks, printers, and other devices, in addition to applications and utility software.

There are two unique features in the PET series that set the PET apart from other personal computers: the graphics capability and the PET bus.

Graphics may be entered directly from the PET keyboard by shifting to uppercase. The graphics keys include straight and diagonal lines, in addition to special symbols and shadings. The PET bus is compatible with an industry standard bus called the "IEEE-488 bus." This bus is used for many instrumentation devices (oscilloscopes, frequency counters, and so forth) and its use on a microprocessor such as the PET has made the PET popular among industrial users of computer systems.

The PET has proved to be a very popular microcomputer, about equal to the Apple in sales.

In this chapter we will be primarily concerned with the PET 2001-8 and 2001-16 computers.

Fig. 4-1. Commodore PET 2001-16 system.

HARDWARE

Minimum System

The minimum PET system is the PET 2001–8 computer. This is essentially the same system as originally manufactured with reduced-size keyboard, integral cassette, and video display (see Fig. 4–2).

This version comes with 8192 bytes (8K) of random-access memory (RAM) and cannot be expanded *internally* to more than the 8K. The newer PET design with the full-size keyboard comes with a minimum of 16,384 (16K) bytes of RAM and may be expanded internally to 32,768 bytes (32K) of RAM. The new design is about $200 more than the original version.

The video display is a 9-inch (22.8-cm) unit attached to the cabinet. As it is manufactured with the PET, of course, it is a black-and-white video *monitor* that uses standard composite video from the cpu logic.

The cassette recorder is a nonstandard cassette recorder that is specifically manufactured for the PET and is integrated into the cabinet.

Courtesy Commodore Business Machines, Ltd.

Fig. 4-2.   Commodore PET 2001-8 system.

CPU

The microprocessor used in the PET is a MCS 6502. The 6502 is a third-generation 8-bit microprocessor that is equivalent in capabilities to the other microprocessors discussed in this book and is also used in the Apple and Atari computers described previously. The clock rate of the 6502 used in the PET is 1 megahertz, allowing about 500,000 8-bit immediate adds per second.

The PET cpu has a built-in real-time clock that provides time-of-day capability.

Memory in the minimum system is 8192 (8K) bytes of random-access memory (RAM) and 14K bytes of read-only memory (ROM). The 14K bytes of ROM memory hold an 8K BASIC interpreter, a 4K resident operating system (nondisk), and 1K worth of diagnostic routines. RAM memory is expandable up to 32K as described previously.

The 6502 microprocessor used in the PET allows 65,536 (64K) bytes of RAM or ROM memory. The memory mapping (Fig. 4–3) is basically divided into RAM and ROM with 32K in each segment to make up a total of 64K. The first 32K of the total is user RAM. Parts of this area are used by the BASIC interpreter or other system programs. Expansion RAM for program storage is located in the 8192–32,767 (8K to 32K) area. The area from 32,768 to 33,792 is a 1024-byte area (actually 1000 bytes) used for video display memory. The area from 36,864 through 49,151 is dedicated to expansion ROM only. The area from 49,152 on is generally system ROM, containing the BASIC interpreter, screen editor, and operating system diagnostics, although a 4096-byte area is reserved for input/output addresses.

The keyboards in the two versions of the PET contain the same keys but are laid out differently. The PET 2001–8 keyboard is shown in Fig. 4–4.

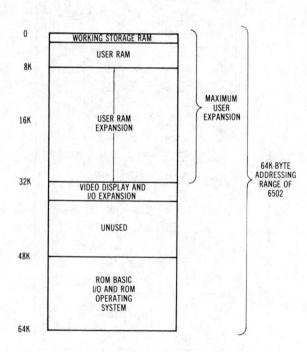

Fig. 4-3. PET memory mapping.

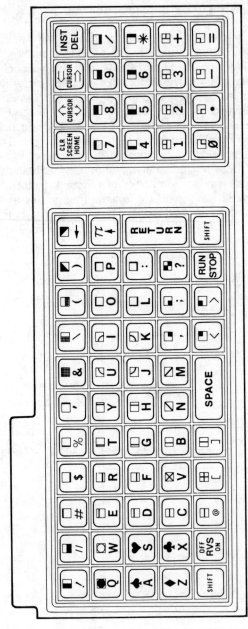

Courtesy Commodore Business Machines, Ltd.

Fig. 4-4. PET 2001-8 keyboard.

Video Display

The video display in the PET is a black-and-white 1000-character display made up of 25 forty-character lines, as shown in Fig. 4–5. Each character of the 1000 characters, alphanumeric or graphics, is made up of an 8 by 8 dot matrix. There is only one display mode in the PET: display of keyboard characters (there is no special graphics mode). There are 64 standard ASCII characters and 64 graphics characters, as shown in Fig. 4–5. There is also a lowercase character set available which replaces the graphics character set. The graphics characters can be combined to draw straight or diagonal lines, shaded areas, and special symbols such as card suits. The RVS key allows for reverse video of any of the 1000 characters on the screen. Automatic scrolling, cursor movement, and blinking cursor are incorporated into the system and controlled by the operating system.

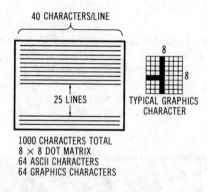

40 CHARACTERS/LINE

25 LINES

8

8

TYPICAL GRAPHICS CHARACTER

1000 CHARACTERS TOTAL
8 × 8 DOT MATRIX
64 ASCII CHARACTERS
64 GRAPHICS CHARACTERS

Fig. 4-5. PET display characteristics.

Cassette Storage

A cassette unit is built into the PET 2001–8 computer, but it is an external option on the full-size-keyboard version of the PET (2001–16). The recording scheme used on the cassette is a nonstandard Commodore recording scheme allowing for high reliability. The cassette drive is modified by Commodore. Standard audio cassette tapes may be used.

Input/Output Connectors and System Bus

There are a number of different connectors on the basic PET cpu unit. One of these is a connector for an optional second cassette unit. A second allows for memory expansion with external memory devices, associated electronics, and chassis. A third is a "parallel user port." This port consists of diagnostic and video monitor signals in addition to eight separate data lines that may be programmed for either input or output. Essentially these eight lines are eight discrete input or output lines that can be used for data transmission between the PET cpu and one to eight external devices.

The last connector is the IEEE-488 bus used with the PET series. The IEEE-488 bus is a 24-pin bus that may be used to connect up to 15 devices to a computer, in this case the PET. The devices connected must be IEEE-488 compatible, that is, they too must have the same interface. The IEEE bus has eight data bus lines that are used for transmission of ASCII characters in asynchronous fashion (not at regular intervals). Eight additional lines are used for "handshaking" and "management." Using this bus allows the PET to interface to measurement instruments, such as spectrum analyzers, voltmeters, and logic analyzers, or to act as a subordinate device to a larger computer system.

Line Printers

Commodore has a tractor feed printer (see Fig. 4–6) that will interface to the PET via the IEEE bus. The 2022 tractor feed printer is a "smart" (microprocessor-controlled) printer that prints on full-size 8½-inch (21.6-cm) paper at 70 lines per minute. It is a dot-matrix type. The printer also has the capability of printing full PET graphics, a very handy feature. A version of the 2022 is available without the tractor feed option.

Courtesy Commodore Business Machines, Ltd.

Fig. 4-6. PET with peripherals.

Although the IEEE bus is very useful for connecting instrumentation to the PET, it limits the number of printers that may be used on the system. There are many more "Centronics-compatible" and "serial" printers than IEEE-compatible printers. Other printers may be used on the PET, but not without some recabling or minimal interface changes.

Disk Drives

The disk drives (see Fig. 4–6) used with the PET are Shugart SA 390 drives. Either one or two drives may be used in the system. The drives are standard mini-floppy (5¼-in or 13.3-cm) drives. The single drive attaches to the memory bus connector of the PET, while the two-drive assembly is connected to the IEEE bus. The single drive has a total of 170.5K bytes worth of storage, while the dual drive provides 341K, about twice as much as many comparable microcomputer systems. Both drives require additional software in ROM (disk operating system) which is plugged into existing sockets in the cpu unit.

Here again, as the disk drives are unique to the PET, there are not very many other drives that will be usable on the system without moderate redesign of interface electronics.

Other Input/Output Devices

Other devices, including a modem, are planned by Commodore for the PET system. There are a number of other devices available for the PET from secondary manufacturers, although not nearly as many as for other microcomputer systems described in this book.

SOFTWARE

PET BASIC

PET BASIC is an 8K interpretive BASIC with floating-point, string-handling, and multidimensional array handling capability. In addition to normal BASIC statement types, PET BASIC has commands that allow communication with all devices on the IEEE bus, the second cassette, and other system devices.

Assembly Language

Assembly-language routines for the PET may be assembled by hand and stored in RAM by using the BASIC "POKE" statements or may be entered using the Commodore version of TIM (Terminal Interface Monitor) for the 6502. The TIM is a minimal monitor (debugger); there is no Commodore assembler program currently available although there are secondary software suppliers that have produced assembler/editors for the PET.

PET Disk Operating System

The disk operating system is an 8K extension to the basic operating system that is plugged into existing ROM sockets on the 2001–16 (or 2001–32) PET (the larger-keyboard version). It provides capability for sequential and random data files on disk and file management functions such as duplication, renaming, and copying of disk files.

Chart 4-1. PET Summary

Model: Commodore PET 2001–8, 2001–16

HARDWARE

Microprocessor:	6502.
Bus, Architecture:	Own bus design internally, IEEE-488 bus externally.
Keyboard:	Integral keyboard. Full size on -16, scaled down on -8.
Television Monitor:	Built-in black-and-white monitor.
Cassette Recorder:	Built-in on -8, external option on -16.
Line Printer:	70 line-per-minute dot matrix printer for full-size paper.
Disk Drives:	Mini-floppy drives. One or two at 170.5K bytes/drive.
Modem:	Planned.
Other Peripheral Devices:	Available by other manufacturers.
Serial, Parallel Ports:	Parallel user port.

SOFTWARE

BASIC Interpreter:	8K resident BASIC interpreter.
Assembly Language:	Machine language though POKE or minimal monitor.
Other Languages:	None.
Disk Operating System:	ROM-based, provided with disk drives.
Utility Programs:	Some.
Applications Programs:	Many available from Commodore or other sources.
User Group Activity:	Some in metropolitan areas.
Publications:	Minimal.
Warranties, Repair:	90 days. Local service available.

Application Programs

As there are a large number of PETs in use, there are a correspondingly large number of applications programs available. Commodore offers business, educational, and game programs for the PET, and secondary software suppliers have developed many others. Currently there are not many large-scale business-oriented programs from either source, however.

WARRANTIES AND SERVICE

The PET versions come with a 90-day warranty on parts and labor. Service is available from the factory or at a small number of locations in metropolitan areas.

PUBLICATIONS

The *CBM User Manual* is a well-written manual that covers hardware and software aspects of the PET. Other documentation is scanty.

SUMMARY

The PET is a popular, inexpensive, personal computer that has good black-and-white graphics capability. It is particularly attractive to instrumentation applications because of the IEEE bus, or to applications that do not require a large number of peripherals, such as the educational area where many inexpensive systems may be required for tutorial purposes. Chart 4–1 provides a summary of the PET hardware and software features.

5

Cromemco Computers

Cromemco, Inc., is a microcomputer manufacturer that has been producing S-100 microcomputers since 1977. There are currently a half dozen S-100 "mainframe" manufacturers (another, Vector Graphic, is covered in Chapter 10) that produce complete microcomputer systems using the S-100 bus that we will discuss shortly. There are also a dozen or so manufacturers that produce S-100 boards that plug into the mainframes and provide memory storage or peripheral device interfacing.

THE S-100 BUS

The first low-cost personal microcomputer to sell in any quantity was the MITS Altair 8800 Microcomputer. MITS, a small New Mexico manufacturer, introduced the Altair in 1975. Orders for the microcomputer surpassed all expectations and the sales prompted many other manufacturers to produce microcomputers for the hobbyist market.

The Altair 8800 used a "bus" of 100 lines. In physical form the lines were etched onto a pc "motherboard." The motherboard was simply a bus onto which 100-pin connectors were mounted. Small (5- by 9-inch or 12.7- by 22.8-cm) cards containing the cpu logic, memory logic, and device controllers plugged into the S-100 connectors.

Many manufacturers produced compatible boards for S-100 systems offering a user a choice between the mainframe manufacturers' boards and theirs, or in some cases providing functions on the board that were not implemented in the mainframe manufacturers' boards.

The growth of the S-100 manufacturers was a mixed blessing. On the one hand, it stimulated development of small computers. On the other, it created some conflicts between boards of various manufacturers, as the S-100 bus was not completely defined due to unused lines; some manufacturers utilized the unused lines for conflicting signals with other manufacturers.

The situation today is that the remaining S-100 manufacturers are the best of the lot. They are producing high-quality S-100 products that generally have no incompatibility with other S-100 products. In addition, S-100 systems have a standardized operating system, CP/M, that has prompted development of a wide range of applications and utility programs.

HARDWARE

General

Cromemco currently produces two basic products: the Z-2 and System Three series. The basic Z-2 computer system is basically a box (see Fig. 5–1A) with heavy-duty power supply, S-100 bus, pc board, card connectors, and excellent shielding against radio-frequency-interference generation. Within the box there are 21 connectors into which the system cpu board, memory boards, and input/output controller boards mount (see Fig. 5–1B).

The Z-2 System

The basic Z-2 computer system contains a Z-80 cpu board (ZPU) which contains a Z-80 microprocessor chip (see Fig. 5–2). This is the standard cpu board for all Cromemco systems. The Z-80 on this board operates at a clock rate of 4 megahertz, which permits 571,400 8-bit immediate adds per second. The Z-80, of course, is used in many of the computer systems discussed in this book and is a third-generation microprocessor chip with a powerful instruction set. The basic Z-2 is about $1000.

In addition to the Z-80 cpu board, the Z-2 optionally contains memory and input/output controller boards, samples of which are shown in Fig. 5–3. Memory boards for the Z-2 and other systems contain 4096 (4K), 16,384 (16K), or 65,536 (64K) bytes of random-access memory (RAM), depending upon the board. Memory board prices range from about $300 for 4K to about $1088 for 64K. Read-only-memory boards (ROM) are also available. The ROM used in these boards is actually programmable read-only memory (PROM) which can be "programmed" under a system controller to semipermanently "burn-in" a program.

A wide variety of input/output controller boards are available for the Z-2 and System Three systems. Boards that are available allow the systems to be interfaced to *parallel* peripheral devices such as printers, paper tape readers and punches, keyboards, and special instrumentation or hardware devices. *Serial* boards interface the system to serial input/output devices, such as serial printers and data communications devices. A color graphics interface displays images of up to 756 by 484 point resolution, a much better resolution than most of the other systems discussed in this book. The color graphics interface is about $800. Other input/output boards such as a Centronics-compatible printer interface, analog interface, and disk controller board are also available from Cromemco.

There are several variations on the basic Z-2 system. The Z-2D disk computer system uses the same basic chassis and boards as the Z-2 system but adds a mini-floppy disk drive. The mini-floppy allows storage of 92K bytes on each diskette. The Z-2D contains the cpu board, one disk drive, and a parallel and serial interface, and complete disk interfacing (no RAM). It is priced at about $2000. A second version of the Z-2 contains the cpu board, two mini-floppy drives, 64K of RAM, a printer interface, a serial and parallel interface, and costs about $4000 (see Fig. 5–4).

A much more expensive version ($10,000) of the Z-2 offers a "hard" disk drive in addition to two mini-floppy drives. The hard disk drive in this case allows storage of 11 megabytes of data on a "Win-

(A)   Photograph of unit.

Fig. 5-1.   Cromemco Z-2

chester" disk. Access time to the large disk is about 10 times faster (1/20 second) than a mini-floppy.

The System Three

The System Three series (see Fig. 5–5) uses the same basic boards and chassis arrangement as the Z-2 series. The disk drives used in the System Three, however, are 8-inch (20.3-cm) floppy drives that allow storage of 256K bytes per diskette. From two to four disk drives may be used in the system, permitting 1 megabyte of on-line storage. Another feature of the System Three is that RAM may be expanded to 512 kilobytes in eight 64K "banks." This is a powerful feature not found on most other small computer systems in this book.

Cromemco offers a full line of peripheral devices for their systems, including crt terminals, line printers, separately mounted disk drives, "joystick" console with speaker, and other devices.

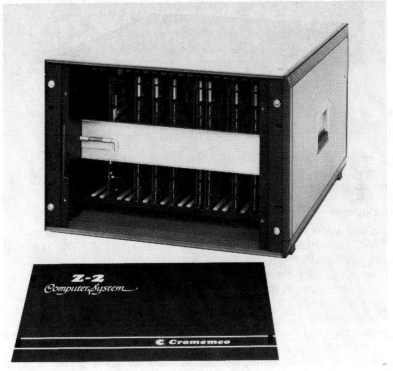

(B) S-100 boards and chassis.

Courtesy Cromemco, Inc.

computer system.

Fig. 5-2. ZPU board.

SOFTWARE

Software is one of the most important selling points of S-100 systems, as there is a great bulk of software that has been developed for microcomputers using this configuration.

Languages

Cromemco has three versions of BASIC: a 16K disk extended BASIC, a multiuser BASIC, and a 32K structured BASIC. The 16K disk extended BASIC is available on 5¼- or 8-inch (13.3- or 20.3-cm) diskettes. It is a "semicompiling" type of BASIC as opposed to an *interpretive* type of BASIC found on other small computer systems. A compiling BASIC generally operates much more rapidly than an interpretive BASIC as the BASIC statement lines are converted to "machine-language" instructions and do not have to be reprocessed on each encounter in the program. The multiuser BASIC is a combination hardware/software package that allows up to seven users to run BASIC programs on one Cromemco System. The 32K structured BASIC runs in a 64K system and incorporates all the commands of 16K BASIC along with a sequential-access method to disk called "keyed sequential-access method" (KSAM) and a "structured" format. The structured format structures the BASIC program in physical and logical layout so that it is more readable and understandable.

In addition to BASIC, Cromemco offers a COBOL and FORTRAN compiler and a "RATFOR" precompiler for FORTRAN. Few other microcomputers offer COBOL, a business-oriented language that is in extensive use in larger computer systems. The FORTRAN package is useful for engineering and scientific applications; RATFOR creates a structured form of the FORTRAN. Both the COBOL and FORTRAN are true compilers, producing extremely efficient code when compared to language interpreters.

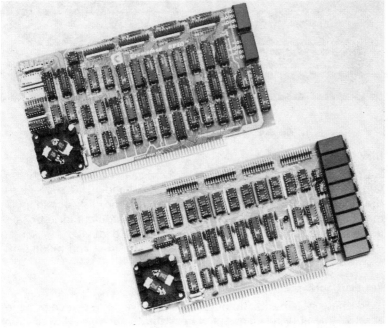

Courtesy Cromemco, Inc.

Fig. 5-3. Typical Cromemco S-100 boards.

Assembler

There is a relocatable macro assembler available from Cromemco for use on the Z-2 and System Three systems. The "macro" capability is a powerful feature that allows in-line code to be generated automatically.

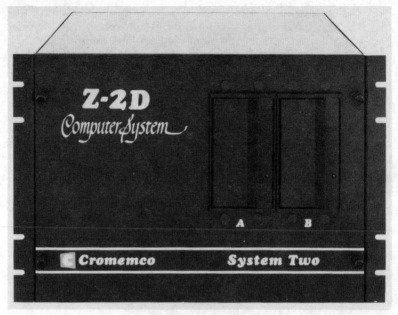

Courtesy Cromemco, Inc.

Fig. 5-4.   Cromemco Z-2D computer system.

Disk Operating System

Cromemco has a disk operating system, called CDOS, which contains many different utility functions. CDOS handles file manage for disk that allows a user to initiate, erase, rename, list, or otherwise manipulate files. CDOS handles all system input/output for every system peripheral device, including nonstandard devices. A screen editor and text editor capability is used to construct and modify system text files, such as assembly source files.

Resident Software

For those systems that do not have disk drives, Cromemco provides a set of memory-resident software. This includes a 16K resident BASIC, a 3K control BASIC, a Z-80 monitor, and a resident operating system. The 3K control BASIC is an integer-only BASIC designed for microcomputer control applications. The 16K BASIC is a version of the 16K BASIC previously discussed. The Z-80 monitor is essentially a debug package.

Applications Programs

A word processing system is available that is used to construct and modify text for letters, manuscripts, or other document preparation.

The Cromemco Data Base Management System processes disk files by performing "sorts" of disk data and can be used to maintain mailing lists, inventory systems, and the like. Other software applications programs are available from secondary suppliers, but not to the extent of the programs available for the Apple II or Radio Shack TRS-80.

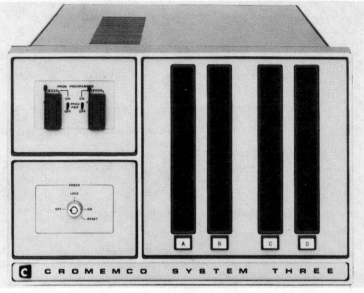

Courtesy Cromemco, Inc.

Fig. 5-5. Cromemco System Three computer.

CP/M

The above software has been developed by Cromemco and is not compatible with the CP/M operating system. CP/M is a standard operating system for S-100 computers that offers a text editor, debug package, a macro assembler, input/output driver routines, a compilerlike BASIC, and other utility software. The Cromemco system will *not* execute CP/M directly unless some software modifications are performed. The advantage of using CP/M is that it offers an extremely wide data base of existing applications and utility programs of every type. There are a number of CP/M users' groups which will provide noncopyrighted software from the existing base of programs.

WARRANTIES AND SERVICE

Cromemco provides the usual 90-day warranty on parts and labor. Repair is available in metropolitan areas or from the factory, but is

Chart 5-1. Cromemco Summary

Model: Cromemco Z–2 and System Three Computer Systems

HARDWARE

Microprocessor: Z-80.

Bus, Architecture: S-100, "box" type system.

Keyboard: None. Optional crt terminals available.

Television Monitor: None. Special display hardware available.

Cassette Recorder: None. Cassette interface available.

Line Printer: Large number available from Cromemco or elsewhere.

Disk Drives: Z-2 uses mini-floppies at 92K bytes. System Three uses large floppies at 256K bytes.

Modem: Available elsewhere.

Other Peripheral Devices: Wide variety of general- and special-purpose interfaces and peripherals available.

Serial, Parallel Ports: Available through S-100 board options.

SOFTWARE

BASIC Interpreter: 16K disk, multiuser, 32K structured BASICs.

Assembly Language: Relocatable macro assembler.

Other Languages: COBOL, FORTRAN, others.

Disk Operating System: CDOS disk operating system.

Utility Programs: Some from Cromemco, many CP/M versions.

Applications Programs: Many CP/M versions.

User Group Activity: Minimal, except CP/M users' groups.

Publications: Generally good.

Warranties, Repair: 90 days. Local service available.

more of a problem than on microcomputers such as the Apple II or TRS-80. On the other hand, the modular type of construction in S-100 systems does permit "spare" boards to be kept on hand to be used while faulty components are being repaired.

PUBLICATIONS

Cromemco publications are generally very good, with complete hardware and software descriptions.

SUMMARY

The Cromemco product line is well suited for the more affluent user or the small business that requires a well-engineered, time-proved, rugged system. It is also excellent for the industrial user who needs the system for control applications, as there is a wide variety of special-purpose S-100 interfaces. Another use is in a multiuser environment, where Cromemco software provides a means to "time-share" the system among seven users. Chart 5–1 provides a summary of Cromemco hardware and software features.

6

Heath Personal Computers

The Heath Company, Benton Harbor, Michigan, offers a variety of electronic kits ranging from simple experimenter's circuits to digital computers. Heath has an excellent name among electronics engineers, electronics hobbyists, and kit builders. Heath circuitry is well designed and their documentation superb.

In 1977, Heath brought out a general-purpose personal computer system, the Heathkit H8. Shortly afterwards, a second computer system, the Heathkit/DEC H11A computer, was introduced. Both computer systems are available as kits or fully assembled. The latest addition to the Heath line is an "all-in-one" computer, the Heath H89 computer, a fully integrated Z-80 computer system that contains keyboard, monitor, floppy disk drive, and electronics in one package.

The Heath H89 and H8 computers are *8-bit* computer systems, while the Heathkit/DEC H11A is a *16-bit* computer system based around Digital Equipment Corporation's LSI-11 microprocessor. The H11A computer is probably the best buy in 16-bit computers anywhere, but is two to three times the cost of the other two Heath systems. For that reason we will be discussing only the H89 and H8 systems in this chapter.

H89 HARDWARE

The H89 is shown in Fig. 6–1. A version of the H89 without disk called the H88 is available at about $1200 in kit form, while the H89 is about $1600 in kit form.

The H89 is basically an integrated computer system with built-in black-and-white monitor. The microprocessor used in the H89 is the Z-80, a third-generation 8-bit microprocessor chip used in many of the other microcomputers discussed in this book. The H89 uses *two* Z-80 microprocessors, one as the main cpu to perform processing, and the second as a terminal processor. The terminal processor independently controls display actions. The advantage of this approach is that the processing functions can be distributed among the two Z-80s rather than having one handle the entire processing. The cpu processor Z-80 has a clock rate of 2.048 megahertz, equivalent to about 292,600 8-bit immediate adds per second.

Fig. 6-1. The Heath H89 computer.

Memory in the H89 is expandable to 48K of random-access memory, and the basic unit comes with 16,384 bytes (16K).

The expansion of memory is accomplished by plugging in additional sets of 16K memory chips. Each 16K of memory is about $150.

The full-size 80-key keyboard includes a "calculator-style" numeric keypad. There are eight user-definable keys (function keys) on the main keyboard that may be programmed for special functions. The keyboard is shown in Fig. 6–2.

The monitor is a black-and-white 12-inch (30.5-cm) display. The display format is 24 lines by 80 characters per line. The 25th line does not "scroll" and can be programmed to display system messages. Characters are displayed in 5 by 7 dot matrix form for upper-

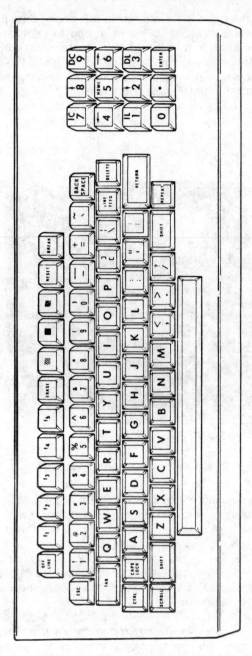

Fig. 6-2. H89 keyboard.

case or 5 by 9 dot matrix for lowercase. The lowercase characters have "descenders" unlike some microcomputer displays that form lowercase characters "above the line." In addition to the alphanumeric display the H89 has 33 "line" graphics characters that use an 8 by 10 dot matrix. These characters permit display of horizontal lines, vertical lines, and other types of graphics lines and patterns. The display characteristics are shown in Fig. 6–3.

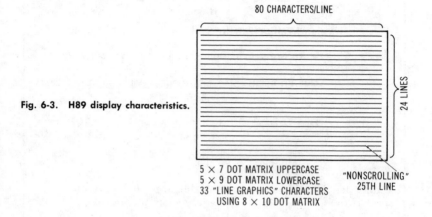

Fig. 6-3. H89 display characteristics.

80 CHARACTERS/LINE

24 LINES

5 × 7 DOT MATRIX UPPERCASE
5 × 9 DOT MATRIX LOWERCASE
33 "LINE GRAPHICS" CHARACTERS
USING 8 × 10 DOT MATRIX

"NONSCROLLING"
25TH LINE

The disk drive is built into the cabinet and is a 5¼-inch (13.3-cm) mini-floppy drive (Wangco/Siemens). Total data storage is 102K bytes on 40 tracks (many other microcomputers use 35 tracks).

The H89 includes a two-port serial input/output interface which can be used to interface to serial printers or data communications equipment (modems). The H88 and H89 include audio cassette interface hardware that allows the system to be used for cassette storage at 120 bytes per second. No cassette recorder is included with the basic system. Line printers and cassette storage are discussed under the H8 System.

H89 SOFTWARE

Software for the H89 system is identical with or similar to the software for the earlier Heath H8 system. Programs written for the 8080 microprocessor of the H8 will execute on the Z-80 microprocessor in the H89, as the instruction set of the 8080 is a subset of Z-80 instructions.

H89 Hardware and software features are summarized in Chart 6–1.

Chart 6-1. Heath H89 Summary

Model: Heath Company H89 Computer System

HARDWARE

Microprocessor:	Z-80 (2).
Bus, Architecture:	Own bus design.
Keyboard:	Integral full-size keyboard with keypad.
Television Monitor:	Integral black-and-white monitor.
Cassette Recorder:	Optional recorder, interface standard.
Line Printer:	Several models available from Heath. Interface standard.
Disk Drives:	Mini-floppy drive built in.102K-byte storage.
Modem:	Available.
Other peripheral devices:	Available from other suppliers for interface to serial ports.
Serial, Parallel Ports:	Two serial ports.

SOFTWARE

BASIC Interpreter:	8K, 12K, disk BASIC, 8080 based.
Assembly language:	Text editor, assembler, debugger.
Other Languages:	None.
Disk Operating system:	Available, provided with disk drives.
Utility programs:	Some.
Applications Programs:	Some business software. Others available from external vendors.
User Group Activity:	Supported by company.
Publications:	Excellent and complete.
Warranties, Repair:	90 days. Local repair centers.

H8 GENERAL HARDWARE

Fig. 6–4 shows the basic H8 computer. Like some of the other systems discussed in this book the H8 uses a "bus board" motherboard. A bus board is simply a large printed-circuit board with system bus lines etched onto it and provisions for connectors on the board. Modules are then plugged into the bus board. Separate modules are used for the cpu electronics, memory, input/output device controllers, and so forth. The main advantage of such a system is expandability and modularity; the disadvantage is slightly higher cost for the connectors and separate modules.

The basic H8 consists of a nine-digit LED display and numeric keypad on the front panel of the system, the chassis with power supply, bus board, and cpu board. The only other item necessary for a functioning computer system is a memory board to plug into the basic system. In kit form the basic system with 4096 bytes (4K) of memory costs approximately $500.

Other modules that can be added to the basic system are additional memory modules of 8192 or 16,384 bytes, a parallel interface module for devices such as a paper tape reader and punch, a serial interface module for line printer or video terminal, and a cassette interface module for cassette and video terminal. Modules range in price from $125 to $400 (for 16K memory).

H8 CPU

The microprocessor chip used in the H8 system on the cpu board is the Intel 8080A. The 8080 is a third-generation microprocessor chip that is probably the largest selling microprocessor in the world. A great deal of software has been written for the 8080. (Not all of it is directly usable on the H8 system, however.) The clock rate for the 8080A microprocessor on the cpu board is 2.048 megahertz, about 292,600 8-bit immediate adds per second.

The cpu board comes completely assembled and contains the cpu and associated electronics to provide output signals on the bus. It also contains a 1024-byte (1K) monitor which allows the user to enter data, display data, and perform other functions from the "front panel" using the keypad and LED panel display.

The H8 chassis includes a built-in speaker which is used as a feedback device for entries on the keypad and for programmable special effects.

Memory

Memory on the cpu board consists of the 1K monitor; this, of course, is read-only memory (ROM) and cannot be used for program storage. Additional memory must be added to the system by optional

Fig. 6-4. The Heath H8 computer.

4K, 8K, or 16K memory boards. The memory mapping for the H8 is shown in Fig. 6–5. The first 1024 bytes are the front-panel ROM monitor on the cpu board. Beyond that, there is a reserved area for system expansion, followed by random-access memory reserved for the monitor (8192). Above this area is the user area of RAM, which may be 57,344 bytes (56K). The user area holds user programs or utility programs, such as the BASIC interpreter.

Front Panel

The most rudimentary input/output device in the H8 system is the front panel itself. The LED display consists of nine 7-segment LEDs that display address and data information. The keypad is a 16-key input device that is used to enter data into the system. The display and keypad, along with the 1K ROM monitor, constitute a complete means for entering and executing short machine language programs into RAM memory.

Video Display

There is no integral video display in the H8 system as there is in the H89. The Heath H19 or H9 terminals can be used on the H8 system. Either requires a serial I/O and cassette interface board for connection to the system. The H19 display is a stripped-down version of the H89 computer and is about $675 in kit form. The H9 crt video terminal and keyboard is an earlier terminal that is about $380 in kit form (see Fig. 6–6).

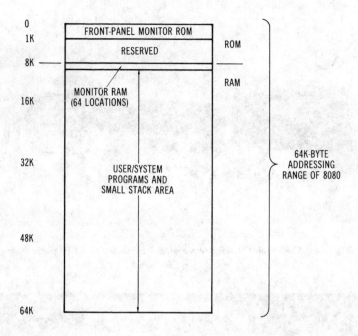

Fig. 6-5. H8 memory mapping.

Cassette Storage

Cassette storage in the H8 system requires a serial I/O and cassette interface board (or four-port serial interface board) and an audio cassette recorder. The recording technique used is Byte (Manchester recording, which allows data transfers to about 120 bytes per second). Two recorders may be used in the system to allow separate recording and playback. Control lines are provided for programmed start and stop of the recorders.

Line Printers

Line printers for the H9 system are also serial devices that must use either the serial I/O and cassette board or the four-port serial interface board for connection to the system. Heath sells their own H14 line printer, the Digital Equipment Corporation LA36 DEC Writer II, or the Heathkit WH24/Texas Instruments 810 line printer for use on the H8 (or H89). Any serial line printer, however, can be used on the system, provided the system has one of the serial boards installed. The H14 line printer is a 5 by 7 dot-matrix printer that prints full-size "sprocket feed" paper. Printing speeds are 135 characters per second at 80, 96, or 132 characters per line. At about $600 in kit form the H14 is one of the least expensive full-size line printers available today (see Fig. 6–7).

Fig. 6-6. The Heath H9 video terminal, H8 computer, and H10 paper tape reader/punch.

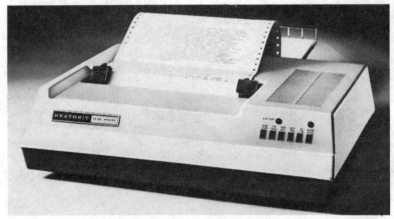

Fig. 6-7. The Heath H14 line printer.

Disk Drives

The Heath H17 floppy disk system for the H8 consists of one or two 5¼-inch (13.3-cm) disk drives. The drive used is the Wangco Model 82 disk drive, a unit that is compatible with the Shugart SA400 mini-floppy. The H17 includes a controller board that plugs into the bus board of the system. Over 204K bytes of storage are available in the system when two drives are used as the drives use 40 tracks on disks (some other computer systems utilize only 35 tracks).

Other Input/Output Devices

Another H8 device infrequently found on current personal computer systems is the H10A paper tape reader/punch. This device reads and punches "paper tape." The paper tape is a secondary storage device that predates cassette and disk storage by twenty or thirty years. It is relatively slow (50 characters per second reading, 10 characters per second punching), but it is certainly tried and true (see Fig. 6–6).

H8 SOFTWARE

Heath BASICs

There are three versions of BASIC available for the H8: an 8K BASIC, a 12K BASIC, and a disk BASIC. The 8K Benton Harbor BASIC is a typical 8K BASIC in that it has a good set of BASIC commands, has floating-point capability, and has some additional commands, such as PEEK and POKE. The 8K BASIC also includes commands for controlling the panel display and for reading the keypad. The 12K BASIC is an extended BASIC that allows string manipulation and additional commands. This BASIC also provides access to the system real-time clock, for time of day, and allows keypad "interrupts." The WH14 line printer is supported in this BASIC version.

The disk BASIC is a Microsoft® BASIC that supports the H17 disk system, has extensions to the commands for string manipulation, and provides file management capability.

Assembly-Language Software

There are a number of Heath software products that allow assembly-language programming on the H8 computer system. A text editor (TED-8) is used to prepare source code for assembly language in addition to providing text editing capability for letter writing, reports, and other word processing tasks. The HASL-8 assembler is a symbolic assembler program that translates 8080 "source" code from the editor into machine language. An extended version of the front-panel monitor console debugger (BUG-8) is a debug package that loads and dumps machine-language programs and allows breakpointing and other debug operations.

Disk Operating System

A disk operating system package for the H8 includes the utility programs described above and file management programs for the disk(s). The DOS includes dynamic file allocation for disk resource management (i.e., "cleaning up" disk space) and copying and back-up functions.

Applications Programs

Heath provides a total accounting business system that includes general ledger, accounts receivable, accounts payable, payroll, and inventory system packages. These BASIC packages are designed to be used on a disk system with video display terminal.

Other applications programs include games from Heath and other suppliers, and a variety of other software available from secondary software producers. The number of programs available for the H8 is certainly not as great as those for systems such as the Radio Shack TRS-80, Apple, and Commodore, but Heath does promote the Heathkit User's Group (HUG), which offers a quarterly magazine and access to a software library that contains applications programs of various types.

Courtesy Heath Co.

Fig. 6-8. Heath publications.

Chart 6-2. Heath H8 Summary

Model: Heath Company H8 Personal Computer

HARDWARE

Microprocessor:	8080.
Bus, Architecture:	Own bus design. Modular approach.
Keyboard:	Chassis keyboard for monitor operation, minimal.
Television Monitor:	None. Optional video terminal.
Cassette Recorder:	Optional cassette recorder and interface.
Line Printer:	Several models available from Heath. Interface optional.
Disk Drives:	Separate mini-floppies store 102K bytes each. Optional.
Modem:	Available, requires serial interface.
Other Peripheral Devices:	Available from other suppliers for interface to serial port.
Serial, Parallel Ports:	Optional.

SOFTWARE

BASIC Interpreter:	8K, 12K, disk BASIC.
Assembly Language:	Text editor, assembler, debugger.
Other Languages:	None.
Disk Operating System:	Available, provided with disk drives.
Utility Programs:	Some.
Applications Programs:	Some business software. Others available from external vendors.
User Group Activity:	Supported by company.
Publications:	Excellent and complete.
Warranties, Repair:	90 days. Local repair service.

WARRANTY AND SERVICE

The H8 and H89 are warrantied for 90 days on parts and labor. Heath has a number of Heathkit Electronic Centers (40 or so) that offer parts and service for the H8 and H89. These are usually in metropolitan areas and many have service technicians that can perform repairs on the H8 system components.

Can you build a kit? If you have put together stereo amplifiers or other kits successfully, then building the H8 or H89 in kit form is perfectly feasible. Heath support is excellent, and the construction manuals are almost foolproof.

PUBLICATIONS

Heath publications are excellent (the assembly and operating manuals for the H89 are on the order of 500 pages). There are complete notebook-style manuals for all hardware and software features of all Heath computer systems (see Fig. 6–8).

SUMMARY

The Heath H89 is a competitively-priced computer system, especially for the electronics enthusiast who likes kit building. The H8 is a good expandable bus-type system that uses the proven 8080. Both computer systems are well designed and well supported by the manufacturer. Chart 6–2 provides a summary of the Heath H8 computer system.

7

Ohio Scientific Computers

Ohio Scientific, Inc., has produced a line of personal and larger-scale computers since 1977. At this time OSI offers a line of computing equipment extending from a computer-on-a-board to a large-scale microcomputer system with 74 million bytes of disk storage.

There are basically four models in the OSI line: the C1P, the C4P, the C8P, and the C3 computers. The C3 is the larger-scale system using 6502, 6800, and Z-80 microprocessors (!) that starts at about $3600 for dual floppy-disk drives, 32K bytes of random-access memory (RAM), and serial interface. This is a competitive system to some of the others mentioned in this book, but we'll limit our discussion to the "personal" computers of OSI— the C1P, C4P, and C8P. These models all use the 6502 microprocessor and are aimed primarily at the personal and small-business markets.

C1P HARDWARE

The least expensive of the OSI computers is the C1P series pictured in Fig. 7–1 with an optional disk drive. The C1P uses a single board, the Superboard II (see Fig. 7–2), which is available separately. The Superboard II is priced at about $280, while the basic C1P is about $350. Essentially the C1P adds only chassis and power supply, so the following discussion will describe both products.

The C1P contains a 53-key keyboard, high-resolution black-and-white video output (monitor not included), audio cassette interface (recorder not included), an 8K ROM BASIC, and 4K of RAM. Quite a bargain!

The microprocessor chip used in the C1P is a 6502, a third-generation chip used in the Apple II, PET, and other computer sys-

Fig. 7-1. The OSI C1P computer.

Fig. 7-2. The OSI Superboard II.

tems discussed in this book. The clock rate for the 6502 is 1 megahertz, resulting in 500,000 8-bit immediate adds per second.

The video display logic generates a composite black-and-white video signal that must be fed into a video monitor (a television without the "front-end" electronics) or must be used as modulation for an rf modulator for use on an ordinary television receiver. The rf modulator is not included, but can be purchased for less than $30. The video display generator logic in the C1P displays both uppercase and lowercase characters from the keyboard in 30 lines of 30 characters each. If an ordinary television is used, this may be reduced somewhat because of "overscan" as the beam goes "off the screen."

The complete character set of the C1P is 256 characters for uppercase and lowercase alphabetic characters, special characters, and graphics characters. The graphics characters include "gaming elements," segments of horizontal, vertical, and diagonal lines, and other graphics configurations. Fig. 7-3 shows the keyboard layout.

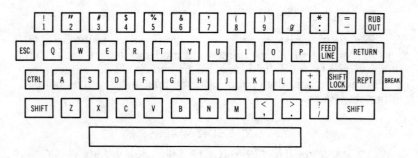

Fig. 7-3. Keyboard layout for the C1P, C4P, and C8P.

The display electronics also provides the capability of addressing any combination of 256 by 256 "pixels" on the screen. This high-resolution graphics is a very powerful feature not usually found on such an inexpensive computer. Fig. 7-4 shows the display characteristics of the C1P.

Memory in the C1P uses 2114 static random-access-memory (RAM) chips for user memory. The C1P basic configuration has eight 2114s for 4096 (4K) bytes of user memory and two chips for 1024 bytes of video display memory. Additional memory can simply be plugged into available sockets on the board. Maximum RAM in the C1P and Superboard is 8192 (8K) bytes.

The cassette interface logic in the C1P uses the Kansas City Standard, operating at about 30 characters per second.

A version of the C1P, the C1P MF, has a single mini-floppy disk drive and is priced about $1000 with 12K of RAM and 8K of ROM BASIC. This system is expandable to 32,768 (32K) bytes of user RAM.

Another disk drive may also be added. A real-time clock, for time of day, is included in the C1P MF as a standard feature.

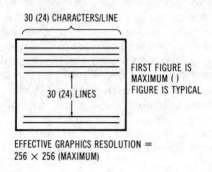

Fig. 7-4. C1P display characteristics.

There are a number of options that can be added to the basic C1P or C1P MF system. A line printer and modem interface are optional items. The C1P MF system can also be equipped with an ac remote control interface for the control of home appliances or the control of other ac devices.

C1P SOFTWARE

ROM BASIC in the C1P and C1P MF is Microsoft™ BASIC and contained in 8K of ROM memory. This is a 6 ½-digit floating-point BASIC with good string manipulation capability and scientific functions. The BASIC with the OS-65DV3.0 disk operating system described below is a digit Microsoft™ BASIC with extensions for disk file manage.

Assembly-language programming for the C1P is implemented by a 2K monitor in ROM. The monitor contains cassette, video display, and keyboard drivers and also has a debug portion that allows the user to examine and modify memory locations and store and load machine language programs on cassette tape. There is no assembler program for the C1P series.

The C1P MF system uses OSI's OS-65DV3.0 operating system for disk operations. This operating system provides named program and data files and sequential and random data file capability. It requires a 20K RAM system.

Other software for the C1P includes educational, game, and utility packages, and business software, such as accounts receivable and payable, inventory, payroll, and mailing list program.

C4P HARDWARE

The next OSI computer in price is the C4P, which sells for about $700 with 8K ROM BASIC, 8K of RAM, color graphics interface, audio cassette interface, and other features. Here again, as in the case of the C1P, the C4P is expandable into a mini-floppy disc system, the C4P MF.

The C4P is pictured in Fig. 7-5. The basic C4P is similar in physical layout to the C1P, with integrated 53-key keyboard in a slope-front chassis. As in the C1P the television may be a monitor or ordinary television receiver with attached rf modulator.

Courtesy Ohio Scientific, Inc.

Fig. 7-5. The OSI C4P computer.

The C4P uses the 6502 microprocessor chip at a clock rate of 1 megahertz, equivalent to 500,000 8-bit immediate adds per second. The C4P is basically a bus-oriented computer system with four card slots internally. The bus is a 48-line system bus that allows system expansion by external interfaces.

The video display generation logic on the C4P uses up to 16 colors. The graphic resolution on the display is 256 horizontal by 512 vertical, about equivalent to a good-quality color television. Excellent high-resolution graphics can be generated because of the large number of points. The alphanumeric display capability is 32 lines by 64 character positions per line. Uppercase and lowercase characters and special graphics characters can be displayed, and graphics and text can be intermixed. The display characteristics of the C4P (and C8P) are shown in Fig. 7-6.

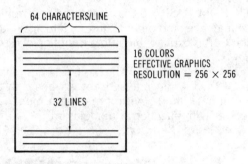

Fig. 7-6. C4P and C8P display characteristics.

The minimum configuration random-access memory (RAM) in the C4P is 8192 (8K) bytes, expandable to 32K. The C4P comes equipped with an audio cassette interface and a number of other extras, including audio output, a digital-to-analog converter for music and voice generation, "joystick" interface, keypad interfaces, ac remote control interface, and printer interface.

The C4P MF (about $1700) is a mini-floppy disk version of the C4P that uses the same mini-floppy disk as the C1P.

Minimum RAM in the C4P MF is 24,576 (24K), expandable to 48K bytes. A second disk drive can be optionally added to the system. A special clock option for the C1P MF doubles the clock rate of the system, allowing 1,000,000 8-bit immediate adds per second.

There are a number of equipment options that may be added to the C4P and C4P MF. Several modems are available for data telephone communications. The modem attaches to an existing "serial" port on the rear of the C4P.

OSI offers three line-printer options that also interface directly to a serial or parallel port on the back of the C4P or C4P MF. The least expensive (about $700) uses aluminized paper for electro-sensitive printing. A second option is a Centronics 779 line printer, while the third is an NEC Spinwriter. Other serial line printers, of course, can be used to interface to the serial port of the C4P.

Two interesting options are the ac remote control set and the home security set (C4P MF). The ac remote control set uses the ac line connected control modules sold separately in department stores. In this case they are computer controlled. The home security set includes a console, fire detector, two window units, one door unit, and demonstration software.

C4P SOFTWARE

Software for the C4P and C4P MF includes the utility and applications programs available for the C1P series. BASIC is in ROM for the C4P and on disk for the C4P MF.

C8P HARDWARE

Next in line is the OSI C8P, pictured in Fig. 7–7. The C8P is a different physical configuration than the C4P as it has an external keyboard, but the bus architecture is the same. The C8P has eight slots internally, compared to the four slots of the C4P. The basic price of the C8P is $895 for a system that has ROM, 8K BASIC, and 8K static RAM.

Courtesy Ohio Scientific, Inc.

Fig. 7-7. The OSI C8P computer.

Another important difference between the C8P system and the other OSI computers is that the C8P system can be upgraded to a C8P DF with two large (8-inch or 20.3-cm) floppy disk drives. The C8P DF with all options is priced at about $2600.

The C8P and C8P DF use the same 6502 microprocessor as the other systems, with an optional GT clock upgrade as in the C4P. Hardware features of the C8P are comparable to the features of the C4P. The models have audio output, a digital-to-analog converter for voice and music, keypad interfaces, joystick interfaces, ac remote control interfaces, real-time clock, home security system interface, printer interface, and parallel ports. Note that some of these features are *interfaces* and require optional equipment, while some features are included in the electronics.

The C8P models can be used with any of the three line printers offered by OSI, the electrosensitive printer, a Centronics 779 full-size line printer, or an NEC Spinwriter impact printer.

Chart 7-1. OSI Computer Summary

Model: Ohio Scientific C1P, C4P, C8P Computer Systems

HARDWARE:

Microprocessor:	6502.
Bus, Architecture:	Own bus design on C4P, C8P, integrated on C1P.
Keyboard:	Integral full size on C1P, C4P, option on C8P.
Television Monitor:	None. User supplied color monitor or receiver.
Cassette Recorder:	Optional. Interface standard.
Line Printer:	Three models available from manufacturer.
Disk Drives:	Available for all three computers. Large floppy available for C8P.
Modem:	Available.
Other Peripheral Devices:	Ac remote control, security package, speech synthesizers, joysticks, others.
Serial, Parallel Ports:	Serial and parallel ports standard on C4P, C8P.

SOFTWARE

BASIC Interpreter:	8K ROM BASIC in C1P. Other BASICs available.
Assembly Language:	Machine language via monitor.
Other Languages:	None.
Disk Operating System:	Available with disk drives for all three systems.
Utility Programs:	Some.
Applications Programs:	Moderate amount from OSI.
User Group Activity:	Some.
Publications:	Fair.
Warranties, Repair:	90 days. Some local service available.

Three options on the C8P models are unique to this computer. A Winchester disk drive is available for the C8P DF that allows 74 million bytes of disk storage. Another option is a telephone interface that has "auto answer," automatic dialing, touch tone communication, and voice recording. A third option is the OSI Votrax voice I/O board that provides synthesized voice generation.

C8P SOFTWARE

Many of the applications and utility programs that are used for the C1P and C4P can also be used for the C8P. The C8P has an advanced small-business operating system, OS-65U, and two types of information management systems, OS-MDMS and OS-DMS. Software is also provided for "foreground/background" processing; in this configuration a background application, such as report generation, can be run at the same time as a foreground process control function or other task.

WARRANTIES AND SERVICE

OSI equipment comes with a 90-day warranty on parts and labor. Service is handled by computer stores in metropolitan areas. Extended warranties are available.

PUBLICATIONS

OSI publications are adequate in the hardware area but could be greatly improved for software documentation.

SUMMARY

OSI computers are some of the best examples of state of-the-art computer equipment available today. The pricing is very competitive for all systems, but the Superboard II or C1P offer an excellent way for the beginning computer hobbyist to get a small system at low cost. Chart 7–1 provides a summary of OSI hardware and software features.

8

The Radio Shack TRS-80s

Radio Shack, a Division of Tandy Corporation, manufactures the Radio Shack TRS-80 Model I and TRS-80 Model II. The TRS-80 Model I microcomputer system is pictured in Fig. 8–1. It is a low-cost personal computer aimed primarily at the home, small businesses, education, and other applications where cost is a primary factor. A more recent introduction is the Radio Shack Model II Computer. The Model II expands on the features of the Model I and offers higher processor speeds, more memory storage (64K bytes), and more disk storage. The *minimum* Model II system is about equivalent to a four-disk-drive Model I. As the Model II is priced starting at about $3500, we'll be talking primarily about the Model I in this section; the Model I starts at a more conservative $500.

The Model I (Fig. 8–1) was introduced in late 1977. Over 100,000 Model Is were sold during the first 18 months. Current sales make the TRS-80 Model I the largest selling computer system of any personal or commercial system, including IBM systems! Part of the reason for the success of the Model I is the large network of Radio Shack retail stores. Radio Shack has not simply rested on its laurels, however, as the TRS-80 product line has been continually updated and expanded to provide all kinds of hardware and software products.

HARDWARE

Minimum System

The minimum system of the TRS-80 Model I is shown in Fig. 8–2. It consists of three units: the cpu/keyboard unit, a video display, and a cassette recorder. The video display is a black-and-white unit manufactured for the TRS-80 and is a video monitor *sans* "front-end" electronics for television reception. The video going to the monitor is "standard" composite video and does not require a video modulator. The cassette recorder is a standard audio cassette recorder, basically unmodified for the TRS-80.

Courtesy Radio Shack, Div. of Tandy Corp.

Fig. 8-1. The Radio Shack TRS-80 Model I computer.

Courtesy Radio Shack, Div. of Tandy Corp.

Fig. 8-2. Minimum TRS-80 Model I system.

The cpu/keyboard consists of two parts, which are integrated into one unit: a full-size keyboard with numeric pad, and a printed-circuit board containing the cpu and associated logic, memory, and input/output logic for the video display, cassette recorder, and system bus.

As the cassette and video display are essentially standard devices that have been adapted for computer use, we'll look at the cpu/keyboard unit components in more detail.

CPU

The cpu and keyboard of the TRS-80 are shown in Fig. 8–3. The cpu uses a Z-80 microprocessor chip. The Z-80 is an 8-bit microprocessor that is an upgrade of the earlier 8080 microprocessor. It is comparable to the other microprocessors described in this book, as it is a third-generation microprocessor chip with a large general-purpose instruction repertoire, high-speed clock, and 8-bit processing of data.

Courtesy Radio Shack, Div. of Tandy Corp.

Fig. 8-3. TRS-80 Model I cpu and keyboard.

The clock rate of the Z-80 is about 1.78 megahertz, allowing about 254,300 8-bit immediate adds per second.

Memory in the minimum system is 4096 bytes of random-access memory (RAM) and 4096 bytes of read-only memory (ROM), as shown in Fig. 8–4. The ROM contains a BASIC interpreter program called Level I BASIC, which is a useful subset of the BASIC language we discussed earlier. The 4K of RAM is used to store user BASIC (or assembly-language) programs which can be entered from the keyboard and saved or loaded from cassette tape.

Both ROM and RAM memory on the cpu board may be expanded. Up to 16K of additional RAM may be added to increase the area available for storage of user programs. This expansion is handled by simply plugging in a 4116 dynamic RAM chips in place of the 4K RAM chips and changing "strapping" on a plug-in device. The additional RAM may be added by Radio Shack or by the user if he or she has access to comparable memory devices.

ROM may be expanded by installing Level II BASIC in place of the more rudimentary Level I BASIC. This must be an addition installed by Radio Shack. The Level II BASIC requires 12K of ROM and is contained in two or three chips that replace the 4K ROM of Level I BASIC.

The Z-80 microprocessor used in the TRS-80 allows for a 64K (65,536 bytes) of memory addressing. As shown in Fig. 8–4 the first 12K bytes in the system are dedicated to ROM containing the BASIC interpreter program. The 16K bytes from 16,384 to 32,768 are user program RAM installed in the cpu. The area from 12,288 to 16,383 is not used as cpu memory, but is dedicated to input/output device addresses and video memory.

Keyboard

The keyboard is a full-size 52-key keyboard. The keyboard layout is shown in Fig. 8–5.

Video Display

The video displays 16 lines of 64 alphanumeric characters each, as shown in Fig. 8–6. The total number of characters is 16 × 64, or 1024. Since each character can be held in one byte of memory, the total amount of video memory required is 1024 bytes. This memory occupies system addresses 15,360 through 16,383. Logic on the cpu board continually scans these memory locations and converts the character data in each byte to a 5 by 7 dot-matrix character which is written on the display. This video refresh occurs 60 times per second, and it is completely separate from other cpu actions such as program execution. Much of the logic on the cpu board is devoted to the video display.

A graphics mode allows 128 black-and-white graphics characters to be displayed. Alphanumerics and graphics may be intermixed. This effectively divides the screen into a matrix of 128 horizontal "pixels" by 48 vertical pixels for a total number of 6144 pixels, as shown in Fig. 8–6.

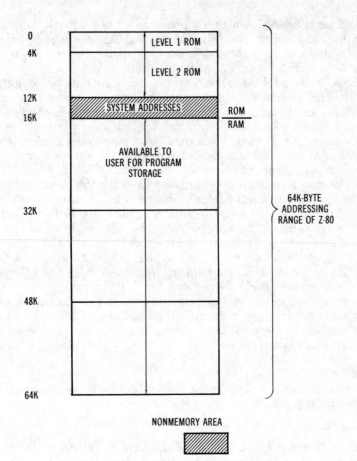

Fig. 8-4. TRS-80 Model I memory mapping.

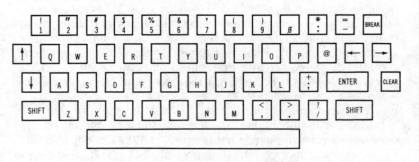

Fig. 8-5. TRS-80 Model I keyboard layout.

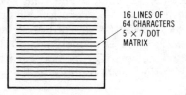

(A) Alphanumeric mode.

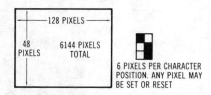

(B) Graphics mode.

Fig. 8-6. TRS-80 Model I display characteristics.

Cassette Storage

Another portion of the cpu board converts data to audio cassette format. Data is output at rates of 250 bits per second (31 bytes or characters per second) for Level I BASIC or 500 bits per second (62.5 bytes per second) for Level II BASIC. The conversion is a combination of hardware and software approaches. A routine in the Level I or Level II interpreter presents the data one bit at a time and controls the timing, or reads the next bit after a time delay on input.

System Bus

The system bus is brought out on one 40-pin connector from the cpu/keyboard unit. The bus signals are derivatives of the signals from the Z-80 microprocessor, for the most part (8 data lines, 16 address lines, and control signals). The bus is used to interface other system devices to the basic cpu/keyboard unit. It is possible to interface other input/output devices by adding additional logic between the 40-pin connector and the device. Radio Shack, however, has an expansion interface available that *contains* logic for interfacing a line printer, up to four disk drives, additional RAM, a second cassette recorder, and a serial device(s).

Expansion Interface

The expansion interface is another "box" that acts as a base for the video display. It contains another pc board with a disk controller chip, printer interface, second cassette relay switching logic, and real-time clock. In addition, the expansion interface contains provision for adding one or two 16K sets of RAM. Adding an additional 16K of RAM increases the user memory area to 32K (see Fig. 8–4); adding two sets increases the user memory area to 48K and fills up the entire 64K addressing range of the system.

Courtesy Radio Shack, Div. of Tandy Corp.

Fig. 8-7. TRS-80 Model II computer system.

Line Printers

The line printer output port on the TRS-80 expansion interface is "Centronics" compatible. Centronics is a line printer manufacturer that has established a *de facto* bus standard for line printers, and, in general, any Centronics-compatible line printer can be used with the TRS-80. Radio Shack sells at least five separate line printers that can be used on the Model I, ranging in price from several hundred dollars to several thousand.

Disk Drives

The TRS-80 uses a Shugart SA400 type drive in their system. Here again, many manufacturers make a drive compatible with the SA400 and there are about a dozen drives that are usable on the TRS-80 with very slight modifications in address "strapping." The SA400 is a disk drive using a 5¼-inch (13.3-cm) floppy disk with about 90,000 bytes of storage on each disk. Up to four drives may be used on the TRS-80, providing 360,000 bytes of storage. The expansion interface is a prerequisite to using disk storage on the system.

Serial Interface

A serial interface board may be added to the TRS-80 expansion interface in a prepared location. The serial interface board provides a means to interface a modem or serial (non-Centronics) printer to the TRS-80.

Other Input/Output Devices

Other Radio Shack input/output devices include a voice synthesizer, a voice recognition unit, and originate/answer modem. Because of the popularity of the Model I, a large number of secondary manufacturers also offer (unapproved) system devices such as color graphics interfaces, large floppy disk interfaces, light pens, and the like.

SOFTWARE

Level I and II BASIC

The primary software for the TRS-80 is, of course, BASIC. There are three versions of BASIC available for the TRS-80: Level I, Level II, and disk BASIC. The most powerful is disk BASIC, which adds about 10 additional commands to the 95 or so commands available in Level II BASIC. Level I is a subset of Level II, with about 34 commands and limited string capability.

RAM Program Storage

The first two versions of BASIC in the TRS-80 are permanently stored in ROM and are always available. Disk BASIC uses Level II BASIC as a base and adds additional commands by loading approximately 5.6K of "extensions" in the RAM area. Any additional programs used on the TRS-80 must be loaded into RAM from either cassette or disk storage. All of the programs described below are either stored on cassette or disk and loaded into the RAM area for execution.

Editor/Assembler

Z-80 assembly language is used in the TRS-80 as all programs of any type, those in ROM or in RAM, are made up of Z-80 instructions.

The Radio Shack editor/assembler program allows assembly of machine-language programs and storage of both the *source* and *object* on either cassette or disk.

Utility and Other Programs

TRS-80 software includes utility programs to renumber BASIC programs, transfer programs from tape to disk, a debug package, and other utilities. Many of the utility programs are written in assembly language.

The large number of TRS-80s has resulted in secondary marketing of virtually any type of utility program required. Many of these are sold by mail or at computer stores. Radio Shack stores carry only those programs officially sanctioned or written by Radio Shack.

TRSDOS Disk Operating System

A complete disk operating system for the TRS-80, TRSDOS, is available for systems with one or more disk drives. TRSDOS includes disk BASIC, disk-related utilities, and a renumber program for BASIC (renumbers BASIC program lines). TRSDOS itself is an operating system that allows storage of programs on disk, storage of data on disk in random or sequential files, real-time clock and date capability, a disk debugger, and general file manage capability (the ability to add or delete various types of disk files).

Applications Programs

A wide variety of applications programs are available for the TRS-80, either from Radio Shack or from other suppliers. Radio Shack programs, many of which are written in BASIC, include programs for business such as mailing list programs, general ledger, inventory control, accounts receivable/payable, payroll, real estate, and statistical analysis.

Educational programs from Radio Shack include programmed instruction for math, algebra, vocabulary, and others. As is the case with other microcomputers in this book, there are hundreds of games available for the TRS-80, many using the video display. Several varieties of chess, including the popular Sargon chess program, are available. In addition, word processing is available for either disk or cassette systems.

Other Languages

A number of other computer languages are available for the TRS-80, including FORTRAN and Pascal. The Pascal package (from a secondary supplier) is similar to the Apple Pascal software. The FORTRAN package contains a FORTRAN compiler, editor, linking loader, and library of subroutines.

WARRANTIES AND SERVICE

The TRS-80 has a 90-day warranty on all system components. Many metropolitan areas have Radio Shack computer stores that carry only computer-related products and offer service for all parts of the TRS-80. Retail stores generally send the system or individual units into the regional computer store for repairs. At this time of writing, there are about 50 such computer centers. Repair charges are conservative, as are allowances for system components added after the warranty has expired. "Foreign" semiconductor chips, modifications, and input/output devices generally will not be serviced whether the remainder of the system is in warranty or not.

PUBLICATIONS

TRS-80 publications include complete technical data on the basic cpu hardware. Technical data on individual units, such as printers and disk drives, is generally scanty. Operating manuals on BASIC, assembly language, TRSDOS, and other software are thorough and well-written.

SUMMARY

Because of sheer numbers of units sold, the TRS-80 offers a credible product with a wealth of input/output devices and programs. Radio Shack computer centers offer fairly rapid and complete service on all system components. Chart 8–1 provides a summary of TRS-80 hardware and software features.

THE TRS-80 MODEL II

The Model II, shown in Fig. 8–7, is a more recent introduction to the Radio Shack computer line. The Model II contains a keyboard, video display, and floppy disk (8-inch: 20.3-cm) in one integrated package. It is aimed primarily at the small-business market. As the Model II uses the Z-80 microprocessor just as the Model I does, much of the software developed for the Model I can be used on the Model II; this includes not only application software, but "utility" software, such as BASIC and a version of the TRSDOS disk operating system.

The Model II is about twice as fast as the Model I in terms of cpu speed. The "clock" to the Z-80 has been doubled in frequency, making all instructions in the Z-80 execute at twice the speed and therefore halving the time for all programs when compared with the Model I.

Another important difference between the Models I and II is that the large floppy disk drive on the Model II holds about 500,000 bytes of data. The larger floppy, then, offers 5 ½ times more storage than

Chart 8-1.TRS-80 Model 1 Summary

Model: Radio Shack TRS-80 Model 1 Computer

HARDWARE

Microprocessor:	Z-80.
Bus, Architecture:	Own design.
Keyboard:	Integral full-size keyboard with numeric pad.
Television Monitor:	Integral black-and-white monitor.
Cassette Recorder:	Provided in basic system.
Line Printer:	Several models available or Centronics-compatable.
Disk Drives:	Mini-floppy drives hold 88K bytes. Up to 4.
Modem:	Available.
Other Peripheral Devices:	Speech synthesizer, voice recognition, others.
Serial, Parallel Ports:	Optional serial interface board provides one serial port.

SOFTWARE

BASIC interpreter:	4K ROM version, 12K ROM version, disk version.
Assembly Language:	Editor and assembler.
Other Languages:	FORTRAN. COBOL, Pascal, others available from other vendors.
Disk Operating System:	Fairly extensive DOS supplied with disk drives.
Utility Programs:	Many.
Applications Programs:	Some business packages, game packages. Many available from other vendors.
User Group Activity:	Very good.
Publications:	Good.
Warranties, Repair:	90 days, Many local service centers. Excellent prices.

Chart 8-2. TRS-80 Model II Summary

Model: Radio Shack TRS-80 Model II Computer

HARDWARE

Microprocessor:	Z-80.
Bus, Architecture:	Own design. Plug-in modules.
Keyboard:	Integral full-size with numeric pad.
Television Monitor:	Integral black-and-white monitor.
Cassette Recorder:	None.
Line Printer:	Several models available or Cenronics compatible.
Disk Drives:	Large floppies. One standard, up to 4. Each stores 500K bytes.
Modem:	Available.
Other Peripheral Devices:	Under development.
Serial, Parallel Ports:	One serial, one Centronics-compatible parallel port.

SOFTWARE

BASIC Interpreter:	12K BASIC.
Assembly Language:	None.
Other Languages:	None.
Disk Operating System:	Standard DOS with system.
Utility Programs:	Many Model I programs will run on Model II.
Applications Programs:	Many Model I programs will run on Model II.
User Group Activity:	None because of newness of product.
Publications:	Good.
Warranties, Repair:	90-days, Many local service centers, Excellent prices.

the mini-floppy, and data can be accessed somewhat more rapidly. Up to three additional disk drives can be added to the basic Model II to provide a total of 2 million bytes of disk storage for the system, all directly accessible at the same time.

A third major difference is that the Model II is a completely new design. Rather than a single integrated motherboard, the Model II uses a "bus" motherboard with 80-pin plug-in modules similar to the S-100 approach discussed for the Cromemco and Vector Graphic microcomputers. This approach has all the strengths and weaknesses of the S-100 structure; expansion is easy, but expensive.

Some of the peripherals used on the Model I can also be used on the Model II—this would include Centronics-compatible line printers.

Chart 8-2 summarizes the Model II features.

9

The Synertek SYM-1

Synertek Systems Corporation is a relatively new company that is producing a "computer-on-a-board" called the SYM-1. The heritage of the SYM-1 relates to another single-board computer, the KIM-1. The KIM was one of the first single-board computers, using a 6502 microprocessor with on-board "hexadecimal" keyboard, audio cassette interface, small LED display, RAM, and a monitor in ROM. The KIM is basically an experimenter's computer and must be programmed in 6502 machine (assembly) language.

The SYM-1 (see Fig. 9-1) is similar in concept to the KIM-1. The basic configuration has an on-board keyboard, audio cassette interface, LED display, RAM, and monitor in ROM just as the KIM has. There are, however, a number of hardware options, such as a crt interface and keyboard, and software options, such as Microsoft™ BASIC in ROM, that make the SYM-1 a complete microcomputer that compares favorably with many of the larger microcomputers discussed in this book.

The SYM-1 is KIM-1 compatible from a hardware and "bus" standpoint. This is an important point because there are many KIM-1 hardware options available from other manufacturers—expansion memory, video displays, and so forth. These devices also work on the SYM-1.

HARDWARE

CPU

The basic SYM-1 (about $250) consists of a 8 ¼-inch by 10 ¾-inch (21- by 27.3-cm) fully assembled pc board, as shown in Fig. 9–1. The only component lacking for system operation is a 5-volt power supply (about $60). The microprocessor which is used in the SYM-1 is a 6502, a third-generation microprocessor used in many of the microcomputers discussed in this book. The clock rate of the 6502 microprocessor is 1 megahertz, permitting 500,000 eight-bit immediate adds per second.

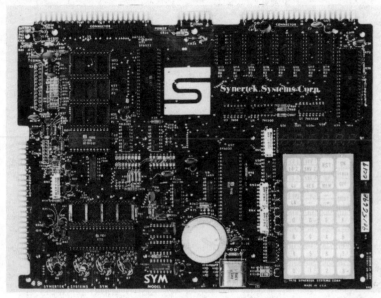

Courtesy Synertek Systems Corp.

Fig. 9-1. Synertek SYM-1 computer.

Memory

The basic random-access memory in the unit is 1024 bytes (1K) of 2114 static RAM. RAM can be expanded to 4096 (4K) bytes by simply plugging additional 2114s into sockets provided on the board. RAM may be expanded even further up to the 65,536 (64K) memory limit of the 6502 by adding additional RAM *externally* on another board. This board is not available from Synertek, but it is available from other manufacturers.

The ROM in the basic board is 4096 (4K) bytes and contains a monitor and operating programs to enable the SYM-1 to operate in the basic or enhanced configurations. The board has an additional three PROM/ROM sockets which could be used to add an additional 6K bytes of PROM or ROM. Additional ROM could also be added via an external memory module connected to the system bus.

Memory mapping of the SYM-1 is shown in Fig. 9-2.

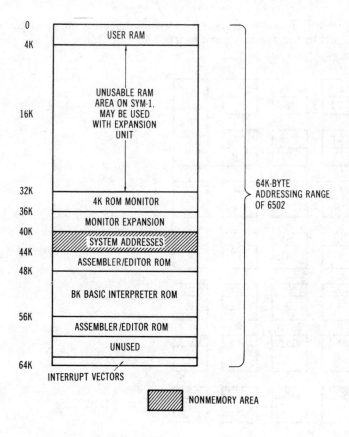

Fig. 9-2. SYM-1 memory mapping.

Display

The basic display on the SYM-1 is a six-digit LED display. The digits of the display are hexadecimal digits rather than alphanumeric, but some alphabetic characters can be displayed by this arrangement, as we all know from using calculators. The display is used by the system monitor program to enable the user to input machine-language commands into RAM, to display or modify RAM, and to implement other debug or system functions.

Keyboard

The on-board keyboard is shown in Fig. 9-3. It consists of 28 color-coded dual-function keys. The SHIFT key provides the dual-function capability. The keyboard is the command input device for a system with no other keyboard or terminal devices attached and can be used to initiate all system functions.

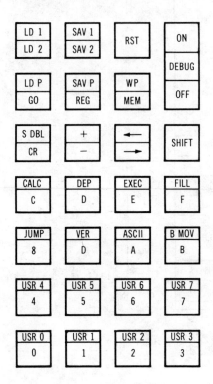

Fig. 9-3. SYM-1 keyboard layout.

Audio Cassette

The SYM-1 board has a built-in audio cassette recorder interface. The original KIM-1 used an interface that would transfer data at about 8 bytes per second, and the SYM-1 has that capability for compatibility with the KIM-1. In the high-speed mode, however, the byte transfer rate is 185 bytes per second. The cassette logic also has remote start and stop capability. The cassette recorder is optional and a medium-priced ($50 or so) audio cassette can be used as an input/output device.

Teletype Interface

An interface for Teletype™ devices such as the ASR33 is a standard connection on the SYM-1. This is a "20-mA current loop" interface that is "full duplex" (allows for simultaneous input and output of data).

Serial Interface

The SYM-1 also includes a serial interface to connect the computer to serial devices, such as a crt display or other RS-232 terminal device. Data transmission rates may be 11, 30, 60, 120, 240, or 480 characters per second. The SYM-1 automatically adjusts to the transmission rate of the device *in* use, an interesting feature. A crt display Teletype, or other terminal device, replaces the keyboard and LED display in displaying and entering system functions.

Programmable Internal Timers and I/O Lines

The basic board includes five "programmable internal timers." These are hardware counters that are driven by a derivative of the system clock and can be used for time-of-day or other real-time-clock functions. There are four "strappable" relay driver or input buffer lines that may be used for external control or input functions on the basic board.

System Bus

The system bus for the SYM-1 (and KIM-1) are related to the 6502 signals. The bus is brought out of the board in the for. 1 of printed-circuit pins. Additional memory, I/O interfaces, and other devices may be interfaced to the system bus by "expanding" the bus so that other boards may be attached.

Other Features

Another feature in the SYM-1 is a small speaker which gives an audio feedback for the keypad and can be programmed for musical tones.

A very interesting feature found on the SYM-1 and no other microcomputer discussed in this book is a built-in *oscilloscope* display capability. This provides the ability of displaying 16 or 32 characters, each character being made up of a 5 by 7 dot matrix. Each of the 35 elements in the matrix is programmable, so that many types of characters or symbols other than alphanumeric data can be displayed. An oscilloscope used as a display device could be any inexpensive single-trace 'scope ($100 and up).

Keyboard Terminal Module

The KTM-2 is a Synertek-designed device that includes a typewriter-style keyboard of 54 keys and a video interface for a standard television receiver.

The KTM-2 requires a 5-volt power supply, which can be the same power supply as is used for the SYM-1. The keyboard is an uppercase and lowercase keyboard which replaces the keypad on the SYM-1 board.

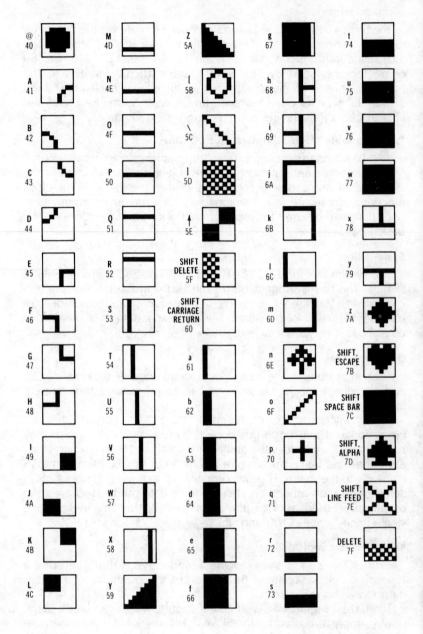

Courtesy Synertek Systems Corp.

Fig. 9-4. SYM-1 video characters.

The video interface on the KTM generates 24 lines of 40 characters each. Another version of the KTM-2, the KTM-2/80, generates 24 lines of 80 characters each. The cost of the KTM-2 is about $350. The KTM-2 can generate 128 ASCII characters, including uppercase and lowercase alphabetics, and can also generate 128 graphics characters. Alphanumeric and graphics characters can be intermixed. The graphics characters are shown in Fig. 9–4.

SOFTWARE

The basic software for the SYM-1 is 6502 assembly language. The original orientation of this microcomputer was towards the experimenter and this remains the emphasis. The 4K-byte monitor in onboard ROM allows the SYM-1 to be programmed in machine language.

Synertek provides a resident assembler/editor/loader for the SYM-1 for use in constructing 6502 assembly-language programs. This firmware comes as ROM and operates in conjunction with the 4K monitor in the SYM-1. The assembler package has a macro capability (in-line routines) and has a *relocating* ability through the loader (programs may be moved anywhere in memory). The package supports source and object files on the system cassette tape device. This is a surprisingly good package for this type of system and, quite frankly, is more powerful than many assembly packages found on much more expensive microcomputers.

A version of Microsoft BASIC is now available for the SYM-1. This costs about $160 and comes "hardwired" in ROM. It operates in conjunction with the 4K monitor and is a full, floating-point, 9-digit, extended BASIC.

WARRANTY AND SERVICE

There is a 90-day warranty on the SYM-1 and other products. Some local repair is available.

PUBLICATIONS

Publications for the SYM-1 are fairly good for a product of this type, but are geared toward an assembly-language user with some knowledge of hardware.

SUMMARY

The SYM-1 is one of the most advanced "computers-on-a-board" in terms of hardware capabilities and interfaces. It is an excellent

Chart 9-1. SYM-1 Summary

Model: Synertek SYM-1 Single-Board Computer

HARDWARE

Microprocessor:	6502.
Bus, Architecture:	Computer on a board. KIM-1 bus compatibility.
Keyboard:	Small control keyboard.
Television Monitor:	None. Optional display driver hardware.
Cassette Recorder:	None. Cassette interface on board.
Line Printer:	None. Can be interfaced via serial port.
Disk Drives:	None.
Modem:	None.
Other Peripheral Devices:	Oscilloscope display logic built in. Optional keyboard display driver.
Serial, Parallel Ports:	One serial port, system bus.

SOFTWARE

BASIC Interpreter:	ROM BASIC interpreter available.
Assembly Language:	Machine-language programming via 4K ROM monitor
Other Languages:	None.
Disk Operating System:	None.
Utility Programs:	None from manufacturer. Others available from vendors.
Applications Programs:	None from manufacturer. Others available from vendors.
User Group Activity:	Some.
Publications:	Good, hardware oriented.
Warranties, Repair:	90 days. Some local repair.

system for the experimenter and/or 6502 assembly-language programmer, although it does suffer somewhat for RAM space on the basic board. Chart 9–1 provides a summary of SYM-1 hardware and software features.

10

Vector Graphic Systems

Vector Graphic, Inc., is an S-100 mainframe manufacturer that initially produced boards for S-100 systems. The board production was expanded into a complete S-100 computer system, and the Vector Graphic system is now one of the best S-100 designs available, having a wide range of functions. (See Chapter 5 for a discussion of the history of S-100 development and S-100 products.)

Vector Graphic's products are aimed primarily at small-business users. The "top-of-the-line" system is the Vector Graphic System B, which includes an MZ microcomputer with two mini-floppy disk drives, a crt terminal, and utility software (see Fig. 10–1). The System B is priced at about $4750. We'll discuss the Vector MZ microcomputer (about $3750) and system components in the following description.

HARDWARE

The basic hardware is a chassis with heavy-duty power supply, S-100 pc motherboard with 18 card slots, and fan. The Vector mainframe is available without cpu, memory, or input/output at about $700.

The Vector MZ microcomputer (Fig. 10–2) is a complete system with cpu, memory, and input/output boards, two floppy disk drives contained within the chassis itself, and utility software.

CPU Board

The heart of the MZ is the Vector Graphic Z-80 cpu board shown in Fig. 10–3. It uses the popular Z-80 microprocessor, as do many of the other microcomputers discussed in this book. The clock rate of the Z-80 is selectable to either 2 or 4 megahertz. The latter, four megahertz, provides the maximum speed of Z-80 operation, of course, at 571,400 8-bit immediate adds per second. The 2-megahertz option appears to be present for use with other manufacturer's boards in systems which are not totally made up of Vector Graphic boards or for slower-speed Vector Graphic memory boards.

Courtesy Vector Graphic, Inc.

Fig. 10-1. Vector Graphic System B.

Courtesy Vector Graphic, Inc.

Fig. 10-2. Vector Graphic MZ microcomputer.

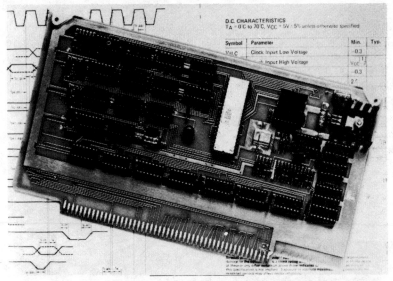

Fig. 10-3.   Vector Graphic Z-80 cpu board.

Memory Boards

Vector Graphic has several S-100 memory boards available. An 8192- (8K-) byte static RAM (random-access-memory) board is available at either 250 or 450 nanoseconds memory cycle time. Another static RAM board provides 300-nanosecond times for 16,384 (16K) bytes of memory. A third board is a 49,152- (48K-) byte dynamic RAM board that uses 16K dynamic memory chips. (In general, dynamic RAM is a more finicky chip with which to design and requires more interface logic. When designed properly, however, dynamic RAM memory is just as dependable as static memory.)

Other memory boards available are two PROM/RAM boards. The first of these provides 2048 (2K) bytes of programmable read-only memory (PROM) and 1024 (1K) bytes of RAM. The PROM would normally contain a monitor for "bootstrapping" the system on power-up or restart. The second PROM/RAM board can contain 12,288 (12K) bytes of PROM and 1K bytes of RAM with an onboard programming capability.

The Vector MZ microcomputer contains both a 48K-byte RAM board and a 12K-byte PROM/RAM board.

Input/Output Boards

Vector Graphic has a number of input/output boards for use on the MZ or smaller systems. The basic input/output boards are the Bit

Streamer and Bit Streamer II I/O boards. The Bit Streamer has two parallel input/output ports and a serial input/output port. The parallel ports on the board can be used to interface with peripheral devices, such as keyboards, paper tape readers and punches, and special devices. The serial input/output port is a standard interface for serial terminals, line printers, and data communications equipment. The Bit Streamer II (see Fig. 10–4) is similar to the first board but contains *three* serial ports. (The Bit Streamer board is used in the Vector MZ.)

Courtesy Vector Graphic, Inc.

Fig. 10-4. Vector Graphic Bit Streamer board.

Two analog interface boards provide the capability to interface analog signals from the external world into the system. The Precision Analog Interface Board contains two analog inputs, eight analog outputs, and a control port. The Analog Interface Board contains an 8-bit parallel port, four analog input ports, and a tone generator. The latter board can be used for interface to joysticks for computer games with sound effects or can be used for analog inputs in control applications.

One of the most interesting boards offered by Vector Graphic is a high-resolution graphics display board. This board is a black-and-white display board that has a resolution of 240 horizontal elements by 240 vertical elements. Each *pixel*, however, can be programmed to display 16 levels of "gray scale," levels from white to black. The board therefore can be used to display a shaded black-and-white digitized picture or other type of display.

Other display boards available are the Flashwriter video boards. These are basically alphanumeric video display boards. The

Flashwriter I displays 16 lines of 64 characters with a 7 by 9 character matrix. Reverse video, block graphics, and line graphics elements and reduced intensity are additional features. The Flashwriter II displays 24 lines of 80 characters with a matrix of 8 by 10 elements. Special characters may be user programmed into the onboard EPROMs.

Peripheral Devices

The floppy disk drives in the Vector MZ are two Micropolis MOD II mini-floppy (5¼-inch or 13.3-cm) drives that allow 77 tracks per diskette. Total storage is 630K bytes per two drives, much more than the usual mini-floppy storage, making the MZ system equivalent to a system with a larger floppy drive.

Vector Graphic offers a "mindless" video display terminal (as opposed to an "intelligent" terminal whose microprocessor performs editing functions). This is a 12-inch (30.5-cm) monitor that accepts composite video and contains a 60-key keyboard. The cost of the terminal is about $775, including the Flashwriter video board, making the package an attractive price for the MZ or other S-100 computer systems.

Other serial peripheral devices can easily be interfaced to the Bitstreamer boards in the MZ or smaller systems, and of course there is a wide variety of serial printers, terminals, and other devices available from other manufacturers.

SOFTWARE

Software available for the MZ system executes under three different operating systems: MDOS, the Micropolis disk operating system, MZOS; the Micropolis/Z-80 operating system; and CP/M. CP/M is a standardized disk operating system that will run on most S-100 computer systems. Because of this, there is available a large data base of CP/M applications software that may be used to advantage on any system that can run CP/M.

Languages

MBASIC is the Micropolis extended BASIC which runs under the MDOS operating system. It is an excellent BASIC which offers disk files and other features. CIS COBOL, a business-oriented language in extensive use in larger computer systems, runs under the CP/M operating system. It provides screen-oriented interaction between the user and program.

Assembler

Assembly language can be used on the MZ system by the use of Vector Graphic's ZSM assembler. Nonstandard Z-80 mnemonics are

Chart 10-1. Vector Graphic MZ Summary

Model: Vector Graphic MZ Computer.

HARDWARE

Microprocessor:	Z-80.
Bus, Architecture:	S-100 bus modules. "Box" type system.
Keyboard:	None.
Television Monitor:	None. Special display hardware available. Terminal available.
Cassette Recorder:	None.
Line Printer:	None. Compatible line printers available elsewhere.
Disk Drives:	Two mini-floppies in chassis, 630K bytes total.
Modem:	Available elsewhere for use with serial interface.
Other Peripheral Devices:	PROM board, analog interface boards, other S-100 boards.
Serial, Parallel Ports:	S-100 board option.

SOFTWARE

BASIC Interpreter:	MBASIC extended BASIC, CP/M BASICs.
Assembly Language:	ZSM Assembler, CP/M Assembler.
Other Languages:	CP/M Languages include FORTRAN, COBOL, Pascal, others.
Disk Operating System:	CP/M or others.
Utility Programs:	Video driver software, others.
Applications Programs:	Data mangement, word processing, other CP/M.
User Group Activity:	Little.
Publications:	Generally good.
Warranties, Repair:	90 days. Local repair, service contracts available.

used, however (most other assemblers use standard Zilog Z-80 mnemonics for Z-80 instructions). An extended monitor provides 23 commands for debugging purposes. The monitor can be set up for the specific system configuration.

Other Utility Packages

EVIOS, Extended Video Input/Output System, and Uni Vid, Universal Video Driver, are two software driver packages designed specifically for the Flashwriter video boards. These packages emulate features found in more intelligent terminals, such as cursor positioning, reverse video, and graphics.

The CCA Data Management System provides sorting of disk files and other utility functions to handle data for mailing lists, inventory, and other data storage and retrieval functions.

The Word Management System is a word processor package that contains its own disk operating system. It provides word processing functions for manuscript preparation, letter writing, and other types of document preparation.

WARRANTIES AND SERVICE

A 90-day parts and labor warranty is included on all Vector Graphic products. Service *contracts* and service centers are available in some major metropolitan areas. Time and materials charges are about $40 per hour if no contract is purchased. Again, because of S-100 modularity, spare boards may be kept on hand for substitution of faulty boards.

PUBLICATIONS

Vector Graphic publications are generally good, with complete hardware and software descriptions.

SUMMARY

The Vector Graphic product line is excellent from a hardware viewpoint. Hardware components are well designed and integrated into the S-100 structure, and Vector Graphic offers one of the best S-100 systems for the money. The manufacturer's software is good, but not a great deal of applications packages are offered. Some of the void may be filled by compatible CP/M applications packages. Chart 10–1 provides a summary of Vector Graphic MZ hardware and software features.

11

Some Other Systems

This chapter will provide a discussion of some of the other small systems that are available. Four of these are older manufacturers, while one, Texas Instruments, is just getting into the small-computer market although they have produced larger computer systems for many years.

COMPUCOLOR II

The Compucolor II system is shown in Fig. 11–1. This is basically a completely integrated microcomputer system with keyboard, color tv monitor (25-inch or 63.5-cm screen), and built-in floppy disk drive. Cost for an 8K RAM system is about $1600.

The keyboard has 71 keys in the standard version, but many optionally have up to 117 keys, including a numeric keypad and special function keys.

The microprocessor used in the Compucolor II is an 8080. This is a third-generation microprocessor (used also in the Heath H8) comparable to the Z-80 and 6502 microprocessors in speed and capability. The 8080 in the Compucolor II runs at 2 megahertz, allowing 285,700 8-bit immediate adds per second. ROM is 16K bytes, while RAM is a minimum 8K bytes, expandable to 16K or 32K. Screen refresh memory is an additional 4K bytes. The system bus is a nonstandard 50-pin bus.

The display is an eight-color display of 32 lines by 64 characters. Two different character sizes are allowed. There are 64 standard ASCII characters and 64 special graphics characters. In the graphics mode the screen is divided into a matrix of 128 by 128 pixels. Crt terminal commands are invoked from the keyboard.

Fig. 11-1. Compucolor II system.

The mini-floppy disk drive is contained in the cabinet next to the screen. Storage on each diskette side is 51.2K bytes, but both sides of the diskette may be used. A second disk drive is optionally available.

The Compucolor II includes one RS-232C serial port that may be used for printer, modem, or other serial device.

Software for the system includes a disk BASIC interpreter in 16K of ROM. The BASIC is a full floating-point BASIC that supports random disk files. An assembler and text editor are available for 8080 assembly-language programming. A number of game and applications programs are available from Compucolor.

Warranty is parts and labor for 90 days. Compucolor is not carried by many dealers and local service may be somewhat hard to find. Documentation is somewhat scanty.

In summary, the Compucolor II has an excellent large display and keyboard functions with high-density color graphics and is a nicely integrated color system for those users that want a basic color system and do not want a lot of add-on equipment. A summary of its hardware and software features is provided in Chart 11–1.

EXIDY SORCERER

The Exidy Scorcerer system is shown in Fig. 11–2. This is a computer system based on the S-100 bus with integrated keyboard and

Chart 11-1. Compucolor II Summary

Model: Compucolor II System

HARDWARE

Microprocessor:	8080.
Bus, Architecture:	Own Design. 50-pin bus.
Keyboard:	Integral keyboard with function keys, numeric keypad.
Television Monitor:	Integral color monitor.
Cassette Recorder:	None.
Line Printer:	None. Available from other manufacturers for serial port.
Disk Drives:	Integral mini-floppy holds 51.2K bytes.
Modem:	None. Available from other manufacturers for serial port.
Other Peripheral Devices:	None.
Serial, Parallel Ports:	One serial interface port.

SOFTWARE

BASIC Interpreter:	16K ROM BASIC interpreter.
Assembly Language:	Machine language via POKE statements.
Other Languages:	None.
Disk Operating System:	Standard.
Utility Programs:	Minimal.
Applications Programs:	Some, game-oriented.
User Group Activity:	Minimal.
Publications:	Minimal.
Warranties, Repair:	90 days. Minimal local repair.

user-supplied black-and-white monitor or television. The interesting feature on the Sorcerer is the ROM-PAC™ cartridge that can be seen on the right-hand side of the unit. The ROM-PAC is shaped like an audio 8-track cartridge, but in reality contains a ROM, or EPROM. The ROM contains the main program language to be used on the system. Typically this would be an 8K BASIC, but assembly language, APL, PILOT, FORTRAN, COBOL, or word processing modules are all products currently under consideration or completed. The advantage of this approach is that a major segment of the 64K memory space does not have to be monopolized by a firmware program; the firmware can be loaded by switching ROM-PACs.

The basic Sorcerer without monitor or cassette recorder and with 8K of RAM is about $900.

The microprocessor used in the Sorcerer is a Z-80 running at a clock rate of 2.1 megahertz, about 300,000 8-bit immediate adds per second. The basic architecture of the cpu is S-100 architecture, and this bus is brought out on a pc board edge connector. An expansion unit can be connected that allows S-100 boards to be interfaced to the basic unit.

Memory in the basic unit consists of 4096- (4K-) byte ROM, supplemented by connection to a 16K-byte ROM-PAC program cartridge. RAM consists of 8192 (8K) bytes, expandable to 32,768 (32K) bytes in the basic unit.

Fig. 11-2. Exidy Sorcerer.

The keyboard is a 79-key full-size keyboard with uppercase and lowercase and graphics characters.

The cassette interface electronics is included in the Sorcerer, and is compatible with two formats—the 30 byte-per-second Kansas City Standard or the 120 byte-per-second format used by Exidy. Many standard inexpensive recorders may be used.

The display electronics in the Sorcerer is one of the most powerful features. The display format is 30 lines of 64 characters, for a total of 1920 characters. Uppercase and lowercase are displayed and the presentation of each character is an 8 by 8 dot matrix. There are a total of 256 different characters that may be displayed. Of these, 128 are fixed, predefined, alphanumeric and special characters. The other 128 characters may be user-defined. (Sixty-four have been predefined initially, but these may be redefined by the user.)

The Sorcerer contains an RS-232 serial I/O port that provides interfacing capability at 30 or 120 characters per second. It may be used to interface any serial terminal, line printer, modem, or other device. There is also a parallel port that may be used to connect to parallel input/output devices such as a Centronics printer.

A combination video monitor and dual mini-floppy disk unit is available for the Sorcerer from Exidy for about $3000. The two disk drives can contain 630,000 bytes.

Software consists of a 4K-byte monitor and standard BASIC. The 4K monitor is within the hardwired (not ROM-PAC) ROM that is on every machine. It contains I/O driver routines for use by the language ROM-PACs. BASIC is an 8K Microsoft™ BASIC with floating point and seven digits of precision. Other ROM-PAC languages are in development as previously noted.

Chart 11–2 provides a description of some of the hardware and software features of the Sorcerer.

In summation, the Sorcerer is a unique design because of the removable ROM and definable graphics characters. It is an attractively packaged system and competitively priced for a basic system.

NORTH STAR HORIZON

North Star Computers, Inc., produces the Horizon computer, an S-100 Z-80 system with integral disk drive (see Fig. 11–3). The Horizon comes as a kit or fully assembled. The cpu board uses a Z-80 microprocessor at 4 megahertz, permitting 571,400 8-bit register adds per second. The basic Horizon comes with the cpu board, a 32K RAM board, disk controller board, one mini-disk drive, two serial I/O interfaces, an 8-bit parallel I/O interface, and all chassis components including fan. The price is about $2000 for the kit form or $2315 for the assembled version.

Chart 11-2. Exidy Sorcerer Summary

Model: Exidy, Inc., Sorcerer Computer

HARDWARE

Microprocessor:	Z-80.
Bus, Architecture:	S-100 bus externally.
Keyboard:	Integral full-size keyboard with numeric pad.
Television Monitor:	None. User-provided monitor or television.
Cassette Recorder:	Optional. Cassette interface standard.
Line Printer:	None. Available from other manufacturers for serial interface.
Disk Drives:	Available as dual mini-floppy with monitor.
Modem:	None. Available for serial port.
Other Peripheral Devices:	None. Other manufacturers units will interface to serial port.
Serial, Parallel Ports:	One serial port, one parallel port.

SOFTWARE

BASIC Interpreter:	8K BASIC interpreter or plug-in ROM-PAC.
Assembly Language:	Machine language via 4K monitor, assembly language via ROM-PAC.
Other Languages:	Under development.
Disk Operating System:	Supplied with disk drives.
Utility Programs:	Minimal.
Applications Programs:	Minimal.
User Group Activity:	Minimal.
Publications:	Fair.
Warranties, Repair:	90 days. Some local repair.

Fig. 11-3. North Star Horizon.

The mini-floppy disk drive may be purchased as a "double-density" or "quad-density" drive. The double-density drive can store 180K bytes. The quad-density drive uses both sides of the disk and can therefore store 360K bytes per diskette.

Two drives will fit in the Horizon cabinet, while a third and fourth drive are available in a separate cabinet.

Hardware options include a hardware floating-point board, a crt terminal, and character and line printers. The hardware floating-point board speeds up floating-point operations by a factor of 25 times or so and is a powerful feature not usually found in microcomputers. A SOROC IQ 120 crt display terminal, NEC Spinwriter, and Anadex matrix printer are offered by North Star as peripheral options.

Software for the Horizon includes a 12K BASIC interpreter, disk operating system (DOS), monitor, and a Pascal compiler. The 12K BASIC is a disk basic that provides a sequential and random disk capability, multidimensional arrays, and string operations.

The disk operating system provides the usual utility and disk file manage functions. The monitor program is a 2.5K-byte RAM program that runs in conjunction with North Star DOS. Pascal is a version of UCSD Pascal similar to Apple II Pascal. There is a large amount of applications software from various North Star user's groups and secondary software companies.

Warranty is 90 days parts and labor. Many computer store dealers carry North Star and some provide local service for North Star components.

In summary, the North Star Horizon system is a well-designed S-100 system with excellent disk storage and software capabilities. It has a relatively large number of users and is well supported by the manufacturer and dealers. Chart 11–3 gives a description of the Horizon hardware and software features.

SOUTHWEST TECHNICAL PRODUCTS
SWTP 6800 AND S/09

Southwest Technical Products is one of the original personal computer manufacturers having brought out their SWTP 6800 computer system shortly after the MITS Altair 8800 in 1975.

The SWTP 6800 was a bus-type system that is based on the Motorola 6800 microprocessor. The 6800 is a third-generation microprocessor equivalent in computing power and speed to the Z-80, 8080, and 6502.

The bus architecture of the SWTP 6800 was based on a 50-line bus known as the SS-50 bus. It has spawned a number of competitors that produce boards that will plug into the SS-50 and at least two other current manufacturers that produce complete computer systems based on this bus architecture.

The newest system from SWTP is the SWTP S/09 (Fig. 11–4). The S/09 uses the Motorola MC6809 microprocessor, an upgraded 6800 microprocessor with a larger instruction set and 16-bit instructions. The 6809 has the capability of addressing up to 768K bytes (!) of main memory directly. The SS-50 architecture is used in the system.

The basic S/09 is available either as a kit or fully assembled. A version with 128K bytes of RAM, one parallel port, and two serial I/O ports is about $3000 in assembled form. Additional 128K memory cards are about $2000.

Software for the system includes BASIC, Pascal, and assembler. Other utility packages available are an editor and debugger. The software also includes a multiuser (more than one system user) and multitasking (more than one concurrent task) capability which takes advantage of the partitioning logic of the 6809 microprocessor.

SWTP makes several types of peripherals for use with its system. The MF-68 (about $995 in kit form) is a dual-drive mini-floppy system with separate chassis. Each diskette will store about 90,000 bytes of data. The DMAF2 dual disk system (about $2500) uses 8-inch diskettes with dual heads for access to both sides of the diskette. Each diskette can hold 1,000,000 bytes of data, making the total for a dual-drive system 2 million bytes.

Another peripheral offered is the CT82 terminal. This is an "intelligent" terminal with up to 20 lines by 80 characters per line display in alphanumeric mode or a 184 by 66 pixel display in graphics mode. The terminal performs many types of editing functions by itself (without computer intervention)—functions such as insertion and deletion

Chart 11-3. North Star Horizon Summary

Model: North Star Computers, Inc., Horizon

HARDWARE

Microprocessor:	Z-80.
Bus, Architecture:	S-100, "box" type design.
Keyboard:	None.
Television Monitor:	None. SOROC video terminal available.
Cassette Recorder:	None.
Line Printer:	Anadex or NEC printers available. Others compatible.
Disk Drives:	One integral mini-floppy in chassis, maximum of two in chassis, four total. Each holds 180K or 360K bytes.
Modem:	None. Available elsewhere.
Other Peripheral Devices:	Other devices available for use on standard serial interface or as S-100 boards.
Serial, Parallel Ports:	Two serial, one parallel standard

SOFTWARE

BASIC Interpreter:	12K BASIC interpreter, CP/M software.
Assembly Language:	Machine language via monitor. CP/M software.
Other Languages:	Pascal. Other languages available for CP/M.
Disk Operating Systems:	Standard DOS, also CP/M version.
Utility Programs:	Minimal. Others available for CP/M.
Applications Programs:	Minimal. Others available for CP/M.
User Group Activity:	Some.
Publications:	Fair.
Warranties, Repair:	90 days. Some local service available.

Fig. 11-4.   SWTP S/09 computer.

of lines and characters and scrolling. At $850 the CT82 is an excellent buy for the SWTP 6800 or other systems.

Other peripherals include an audio cassette interface kit and inexpensive ($250) 40 character-per-line printer kit.

In summary, the SWTP S/09 is a much more expensive system than the SWTP 6800, but an extremely powerful one, probably more so than any other microcomputer system discussed in this book. It appears that it will find more use in business applications than as a personal computer system, although it would be an excellent system for the affluent hobbyist. Chart 11–4 describes the hardware and software aspects of the S/09.

TEXAS INSTRUMENTS TI-99/4

Texas Instruments is entering the "home" computer field with their TI-99/4 home computer (see Fig. 11–5). The TI-99/4 is a small computer with integral keyboard, ROM cartridge capability, and color graphics with TI-provided 13-inch (33-cm) color television monitor.

The basic cpu uses a TI 9900 microprocessor. The 9900 is a *16-bit* microprocessor, unlike the microprocessors used in the other small

Chart 11-4. SWTP S/09 Summary

Model: Southwest Technical Products S/09 Computer

HARDWARE

Microprocessor:	Motorola 6809 (16-bit).
Bus, Architecture:	SS-50 bus with plug-in modules. 128K memory.
Keyboard:	None. CT-82 Terminal available.
Television Monitor:	None. CT-82 Terminal available.
Cassette Recorder:	Available.
Line Printer:	Available. Serial line printers may also be used.
Disk Drives:	DMAF2 is dual drive 8-inch floppy at 1 megabyte per drive. MF-68 is dual mini-floppy.
Modem:	None.
Other Peripheral Devices:	Other SS-50 modules offered by SWTP or other manufacturers.
Serial, Parallel Ports:	One parallel port, two serial ports.

SOFTWARE

BASIC Interpreter:	Available.
Assembly Language:	Available through monitor (machine language) or assembler.
Other Languages:	Pascal.
Disk Operating System:	Standard with disk drives.
Utility Programs:	Some.
Applications Programs:	Some.
User Group Activity:	SS-50 (6800) group fairly active.
Publications:	Fair.
Warranties, Repair	90 days. Little local service available.

computers previously discussed. The TI-99/4 has 16K bytes of ROM containing a BASIC interpreter and sound and color graphics programs. The RAM area available for user's programs is 16K bytes. Another 30K of ROM is utilized by plugging in preprogrammed software modules containing applications programs.

Fig. 11-5. Texas Instruments TI-99/4 home computer.

The display format is 24 lines of 32 characters in an 8 by 8 dot matrix in alphanumeric mode. Resolution in graphics mode is 192 by 256 pixels. Sixteen separate colors may be used.

The basic system provides both music and sound effects capability. Five octaves of notes may be programmed from 110 hertz to beyond 40,000 hertz with three-part harmony. The TI-99/4 also has speech synthesis capability with a vocabulary of over 200 words. Optional remote controls can be used for game control or other uses.

Chart 11-5. Texas Instruments TI-99/4 Summary

Model: Texas Instruments, Inc., TI-99/4 Home Computer

HARDWARE

Microprocessor:	TI 9900 (16-bit).
Bus, Architecture:	Own design.
Keyboard:	Integral full-size keyboard.
Television Monitor:	Separate, but standard color monitor.
Cassette Recorder:	None.
Line Printer:	Under development.
Disk Drives:	Under development.
Modem:	Serial adapter for modem under development.
Other Peripheral Devices:	Under development.
Serial, Parallel Ports:	None.

SOFTWARE

BASIC Interpreter:	16K ROM BASIC interpreter.
Assembly Language:	None.
Other Languages:	None.
Disk Operating System:	Under development.
Utility Programs:	Minimal.
Applications Programs:	Many applications programs on plug-in ROM cartridges under development.
User Group Activity:	None because of newness of product.
Publications:	Fair.
Warranties, Repair	90 days. Service undefined.

Peripheral options planned for the TI-99/4 include a 32-character line printer, disk drive, and RS-232 peripheral adapter.

BASIC for the system is a full, floating-point, 13-digit, extended BASIC. Commands are included for color graphics, sound, and music capability. String variables of up to 255 characters and three-dimensional arrays are allowed in the BASIC.

Texas Instruments will offer a large number of Solid State Software™ modules for the TI-99/4. These will range from computerized chess to personal finance and educational software.

In summation, the TI-99/4 appears to be a good home computer for those users who will primarily depend on "canned" software applications, rather than writing their own applications programs. It is not compatible with the needs of those interested in assembly-language programming or computer system experimenters. Chart 11−5 provides a summary of TI-99/4 hardware and software features.

OTHER MANUFACTURERS

There are a number of other computer manufacturers that have not been discussed in the foregoing. Many of these are excellent, reasonably priced systems, and the author does not exclude them on the basis of quality. Some of the small computer systems not mentioned are "computers-on-a-board" that are primarily meant for assembly language or control applications. Others are too far at the opposite end of the range and are too expensive for other than moderate business applications. The author hopes that the systems discussed in this book provide a good basis for some of the most popular small computer systems, and that the reader will obtain enough information from these pages to help him or her in choosing a system suitable for the application.

Appendix

Small Computer Manufacturers

Altos Computer Systems
2378B Walsh Avenue
Santa Clara, CA 95050

Z-80 disk-based microcomputer with S-100 architecture.

Apple Computer, Inc.
10260 Bandley Drive
Cupertino, CA 95014

Apple II 6502 computer. Integrated unit, user-supplied color television.

Atari, Inc.
1265 Borregas Avenue
Sunnyvale, CA 94086

Atari 400 and 800 6502 computers. Integrated unit, user-supplied color television.

Commodore Business Machines, Ltd.
3330 Scott Boulevard
Santa Clara, CA 95050

PET computer. Integrated 6502-based unit with keyboard, black-and-white monitor.

Compucolor Corp.
Intecolor Drive, Technology Park/Atlanta
Norcross, GA 30071

Compucolor II system. Integrated 8080-based unit with keyboard, color monitor, disk.

Computer Data Systems
5460 Fairmont Drive
Wilmington, DE 19808

Versatile 3B system. Integrated 8085-based unit with keyboard, black-and-white monitor, S-100 architecture.

Cromemco, Inc.
280 Bernardo Avenue
Mountain View, CA 94040

Several S-100 Z-80-based larger-scale systems.

E & L Instruments, Inc.
61 First Street
Derby, CT 06418

8080-based experimenter's computer.

Exidy, Inc. 390 Java Drive Sunnyvale, CA 94086	Sorcerer computer. Z-80-based computer with integrated keyboard, user-supplied television, S-100 architecture.
Gimix, Inc. 1337 West 37th Place Chicago, IL 60609	System 68. 6800-based system with SS-50 architecture.
Heath Company Benton Harbor, MI 49022	Several different computers in kit or assembled form.
Inter Systems P. O. Box 91 Ithaca, New York 14850	DPS-1 system. Z-80-based S-100 system.
Midwest Scientific Instruments, Inc. 220 West Cedar Olathe, KS 66061	Several systems. 6800-based computers with SS-50 architecture.
NEC Microcomputers, Inc. 173 Worchester Street Wellesley, MA 02181	Computer-on-a-board using the 8080.
Netronics Research & Development, Inc. 333 Litchfield Road New Milford, CT 06776	Elf II computer. Low-cost "computer-on-a-board" using the RCA COSMAC 1802.
North Star Computers, Inc. 1440 Fourth Street Berkeley, CA 94710	Horizon system. Z-80-based system with integral disc and S-100 architecture.
Ohio Scientific, Inc. 1333 S. Chillicothe Road Aurora, OH 44202	Several computer systems. Three based on 6502 with color display on user-supplied television.
Radio Shack A Divison of Tandy Corp. 1600 One Tandy Center Fort Worth, TX 76102	TRS-80 Models I and II. Z-80-based computers with integrated keyboard, black-and-white monitor, and disk.
RCA Corporation VIP Marketing New Holland Avenue Lancaster, PA 17604	COSMAC VIP. Low-cost experimenter's computer, fully assembled, based on RCA COSMAC 1802.
Southwest Technical Products 219 W. Rhapsody San Antonio, TX 78216	SWTP 6800. 6800-based system with SS-50 architecture.
Synertek Systems Corp. 150 S. Wolfe Road Sunnyvale, CA 94086	SYM-1. Computer-on-a-board 6502-based system.

Texas Instruments, Inc.
Digital Systems Division
P.O. Box 1444
Houston, TX 77001

TI-99/4. Home TI-9900 based computer with integrated keyboard, separate color monitor.

Vector Graphic, Inc.
31364 Via Colinas
Westlake Village, CA 91361

Several systems. Z-80-based computers with S-100 architecture.

Why *Isn't* Johnny Crying?